The Perennial Philosophy

Series

About This Book

"Joseph Epes Brown, perhaps best known for *The Sacred Pipe* ... spent a lifetime helping to situate the religious heritage of the American Indians within the context of the world's religious traditions. *The Spiritual Legacy of the American Indian* is the collection of his essays written over the period of twenty years, the record of his efforts to bring American Indian religions their due recognition and respect."
    —Leonard J. Biallas, Quincy College

"This collection of essays is a fine sequel to Huston Smith's *The Religions of Man*. Joseph Epes Brown offers a vivid portrait of American Indian spirituality and argues that it should be studied alongside the great world religions.... He has accomplished the difficult task of providing a strong introduction to one of the world's great living religious traditions."
    —Amanda Porterfield, Syracuse University

"Brown, a long-time student of Native American religion, has offered the public a brief, highly readable introduction to American Indian spirituality as claiming a place among the great religions of the world. This short work deserves to be in the collection of any student interested in American Indian life."
    —Carl F. Starkloff, S.J, Regis College, Toronto School of Theology

"America has not produced another scholar of the Native American traditions who combined in himself, as did Joseph Brown, profound spiritual and intellectual insight and traditional understanding, the deepest empathy for those traditions, nobility of character and generosity towards his students and everyone else who wanted to benefit from his unrivalled knowledge of the spiritual legacy of the first inhabitants of this continent."
    —Seyyed Hossein Nasr, George Washington University

World Wisdom
The Library of Perennial Philosophy

The Library of Perennial Philosophy is dedicated to the exposition of the timeless Truth underlying the diverse religions. This Truth, often referred to as the *Sophia Perennis*—or Perennial Wisdom—finds its expression in the revealed Scriptures as well as the writings of the great sages and the artistic creations of the traditional worlds.

The Spiritual Legacy of the American Indian: Commemorative Edition with Letters While Living with Black Elk appears as one of our selections in the Perennial Philosophy series.

The Perennial Philosophy Series

In the beginning of the twentieth century, a school of thought arose which has focused on the enunciation and explanation of the Perennial Philosophy. Deeply rooted in the sense of the sacred, the writings of its leading exponents establish an indispensable foundation for understanding the timeless Truth and spiritual practices which live in the heart of all religions. Some of these titles are companion volumes to the Treasures of the World's Religions series, which allows a comparison of the writings of the great sages of the past with the perennialist authors of our time.

Joseph Epes Brown and Black Elk, Pine Ridge 1947

THE SPIRITUAL LEGACY
OF THE AMERICAN INDIAN

Commemorative Edition with Letters
While Living with Black Elk

Joseph Epes Brown

Edited by

Marina Brown Weatherly
Elenita Brown &
Michael Oren Fitzgerald

Introduction by

Åke Hultkrantz

World Wisdom

The Spiritual Legacy of the American Indian
Commemorative Edition with Letters While Living with Black Elk
© 2007 World Wisdom, Inc.

Most Recent Printing Indicated by the last digit below:

10 9 8 7 6 5 4 3 2

Library of Congress Cataloging-in-Publication Data

Brown, Joseph Epes.
  The spiritual legacy of the American Indian : commemorative edition with let-
ters while living with Black Elk / Joseph Epes Brown ; edited by Marina Brown
Weatherly Michael Oren Fitzgerald & Elenita Brown ; introduction by Åke
Hultkrantz.
    p. cm. -- (The perennial philosophy series)
  Includes bibliographical references and index.
  ISBN-13: 978-1-933316-36-9 (pbk. : alk. paper)
  ISBN-10: 1-933316-36-5 (pbk. : alk. paper) 1. Indians of North America--Great
Plains--Religion. 2. Indian cosmology--Great Plains. 3. Indian mythology--Great
Plains. I. Weatherly, Marina Brown, 1957- II. Fitzgerald, Michael Oren, 1949- III.
Brown, Elenita. IV. Title.
  E78.G73 B7 2007
  299.7'98--dc22

                                                                          2006100071

Cover: Black Elk, 1948
Photograph by Joseph E. Brown

Printed on acid-free paper in Canada.

For information address World Wisdom, Inc.
P.O. Box 2682, Bloomington, Indiana 47402-2682

www.worldwisdom.com

To *Hehaka Sapa* (Black Elk)
who was a living representative of the deepest
spiritual wisdom of the Lakota people;
and to the distinguished Swedish scholar
Åke Hultkrantz
who has developed the special methodologies by
which American Indian religions are seen in their
full cultural and historical contexts

Portions of the royalties from this book go to the
American Indian College Fund

CONTENTS

EDITORS' PREFACE

Joseph Epes Brown's *The Spiritual Legacy of the American Indian* was originally published by Crossroad Publishing in 1982 and has been out of print for several years. Author, professor, and a foremost authority on American Indian traditions, Joseph Brown selected his most important articles from the first thirty-seven years of his work to produce the original edition of this book. The selection of articles includes "The Spiritual Legacy of the American Indian," a seminal article that provides an overview and summary of Brown's understanding of American Indian spirituality and that also inspired the title for the book.

This classic work of American Indian spirituality is Joseph Brown's second most important book after *The Sacred Pipe: Black Elk's Account of the Seven Rites of the Oglala Sioux*, which is one of the most important accounts of American Indian spirituality ever published due to Black Elk's stature as one of the most eminent American Indian spiritual leaders of the twentieth century. *The Spiritual Legacy of the American Indian* is invaluable for a complete understanding of American Indian spirituality because it provides insights into the thought of American Indian spiritual leaders from someone who traveled and lived among those leaders. As Åke Hultkrantz wrote about this book, "Joseph Brown's evaluations constitute the ideological frame of facts which are reliable and which, I may add, reveal religious details that many other field workers have ignored."

This Commemorative Edition contains several important new additions:

- Unpublished letters Brown wrote while living with Black Elk
- Photographs, some previously unpublished, of American Indian spiritual leaders
- An introduction by Åke Hultkrantz
- A preface by the co-editors
- A complete bibliography of Brown's writings
- A four page biography of Joseph Brown's life

The Appendix of unpublished letters will be essential to anyone who wants a complete picture of Black Elk's life, as they reveal important, previously unavailable, details about Black Elk's life from a first-hand observer. Joseph Epes Brown wrote these letters during 1947, 1948, and 1954.[1] Most of the letters dated 1947 and 1948 were

---

[1] Personal references have been deleted and some of Dr. Brown's writings have been

written during the time that Dr. Brown was living with Black Elk and was recording *The Sacred Pipe: Black Elk's Account of the Seven Sacred Rites of the Oglala Sioux*. These letters contain contemporaneous accounts of Black Elk's life and beliefs over a period of two years and are historically important for several reasons. First, in recent years various theories have been presented about the extent to which Black Elk was a sincere Catholic and the extent to which he remained faithful to his ancestral Lakota traditions throughout the later years of his life.[2] Brown's letters shed important new light on this ongoing debate by providing important first-hand accounts of Black Elk's relationship to each of these two different spiritual traditions.

These letters also provide a final chapter to Black Elk's life because of their sharp contrast to the despair in Black Elk's closing words in *Black Elk Speaks*, ". . . you see me now a pitiful old man who has done nothing, for the nation's hoop is broken and scattered. There is no center any longer, and the sacred tree is dead."[3] These words were spoken at a time when most American Indian traditional ceremonies were still outlawed by the U.S. Government[4] and the majority of Lakota youth were not aware of their ancestral spiritual traditions. Joseph Brown's arrival in 1947 was a catalyst that provided Black Elk the practical support to work toward perpetuating his ancestral spiritual traditions, both through the recording of his account of the seven sacred rites of

---

rearranged to facilitate reader comprehension. All of the footnotes in the Appendix are editors' notes to provide further context for the reader.

[2] The following books offer different interpretations and theories on these points: Raymond J. DeMallie, ed. *The Sixth Grandfather: Black Elk's Teachings Given to John G. Neihardt* (Lincoln: University of Nebraska Press, 1984); Paul B. Steinmetz, *Pipe, Bible, and Peyote Among the Oglala Lakota*, rev. ed. (Knoxville: University of Tennessee Press, 1990); Julian Rice, *Black Elk's Story: Distinguishing Its Lakota Purpose* (Albuquerque: University of New Mexico Press, 1991); Michael F. Steltenkamp, *Black Elk: Holy Man of the Oglala* (Norman: University of Oklahoma Press, 1992); Clyde Holler, *Black Elk's Religion: The Sun Dance and Lakota Catholicism* (Syracuse, N.Y.: Syracuse University Press, 1995); and Damian Costello, *Black Elk, Colonialism and Lakota Catholicism* (Maryknoll: Orbis, 2005).

[3] John Neihardt, *Black Elk Speaks* (Lincoln: University of Nebraska Press, 1932). DeMallie's *The Sixth Grandfather* contains transcriptions of the actual interviews with Black Elk, which verify Black Elk's comment that he had not yet done anything to perpetuate his ancestral traditions. Those transcriptions also document Black Elk's prayer that *Wakan-Tanka* will restore the Lakota ancestral spiritual traditions.

[4] Beginning in 1884 various acts of Congress outlawed almost all traditional Native ceremonies. The American Indian Reorganization Act of 1934 repealed those prohibitions. *Black Elk Speaks* was recorded by Neihardt in 1931.

the Lakota and through Black Elk's efforts to reestablish an "Order of the Pipe" for his tribe. History records the successful reemergence of the Lakota spiritual traditions, which are vibrant today on every Lakota reservation. This achievement was the result of efforts by many Lakota spiritual leaders, but there is no doubt that Black Elk's work with Joseph Brown was an integral part of the overall success of this reemergence. The importance of *The Sacred Pipe* to the resurrection and perpetuation of these ancestral traditions is well known. The Appendix of letters clearly documents a largely unrecognized effort by Black Elk to meet with many tribal elders in order to actively stimulate the process of spiritual renewal for the Lakota people. Black Elk recognized Joseph Brown's integral role in facilitating his work when the Lakota holy man said to Brown at the time of his arrival in 1947 that his coming was a "Godsend."[5] *The Sacred Pipe* and these letters therefore document a final chapter in Black Elk's life that fulfilled the great vision of his youth and helped make the sacred tree of the Lakota people bloom again.

Finally, these letters demonstrate Joseph Brown's close personal relationship with not only Black Elk, but also with other spiritual leaders of the Lakota, Crow, Shoshone, Hopi, and Blackfeet Nations. Several of the men Brown describes in these letters were among the most important spiritual leaders in their respective tribes. Joseph Epes Brown was not a scholar who lived in an ivory tower, but a man who strove to understand American Indian spiritual traditions around the campfires directly from tribal spiritual leaders until his death in 2000.

This Commemorative Edition is a tribute to the life and career of Joseph Epes Brown and has been prepared by three people who knew and loved him: Elenita Brown, his wife since 1952, Marina Brown Weatherly, his eldest daughter, and Michael Oren Fitzgerald, his graduate teaching assistant for two years when Joseph Brown was a professor at Indiana University. Each of the co-editors shares Joseph Brown's respect for the American Indians and each of them has also spent extended amounts of time living among Plains Indian tribes. Their unprecedented access to private archives has made this work possible.

The far-reaching consequences of Joseph Brown's influence as a professor of religious studies continue to reverberate through the work of many of his students and colleagues who are currently teaching about the American Indian traditions or who have written books about

---

[5] For the complete quotation see p. 99.

American Indian spirituality.

All of the photographs are portraits of people mentioned in the letters, including Brown, and allow the letters to come to life. The introduction by Åke Hultkrantz, Brown's long-time friend and his professor at the University of Stockholm, provides important insights into Joseph Brown's unique contribution to the understanding of American Indian spiritual traditions. And the new four-page biography of Joseph Brown's life provides a more complete portrait of a man who was instrumental in the preservation, perpetuation, and understanding of American Indian spiritual traditions.

ELENITA BROWN   Stevensville, Montana
MARINA BROWN WEATHERLY   Stevensville, Montana
MICHAEL OREN FITZGERALD   Bloomington, Indiana

September 2006

PREFACE

The chapters of this volume represent a selection of studies originally prepared for journals and conferences. Due to the diversity of the publications and audiences, as well as the time span involved, it could well be asked what presiding or connective principles would give unity and cohesion to the total statement of this book. I can suggest two responses to this question, one historical and the other internal to the subject matter itself.

All of the chapter topics, which have been selected for the general reader, come out of a longstanding concern to develop the means by which selected and interrelated perspectives from the disciplines of cultural anthropology and the history of religions could be used to situate Native American spiritual heritages within the context of world religious traditions. This approach has made clear the necessity for reevaluating still existing Native American primal traditions, and in the process, to free them from outmoded prejudices that are revealed in such loaded polar terms as primitive and progressive, backward and developed, literate and illiterate, among others. All of the chapters of this book elaborate on this central concern by means of a wide range of specific examples drawn from selected Native American cultures.

A second factor contributing to the unity of this book is found in another different approach to the study and understanding of American Indian religions. It has now become abundantly clear that it is a fundamental and universal characteristic of Native American cultures, as indeed of all primal or primitive cultures, that "religion"—there is no equivalent word for this in any American Indian language—is not a separate category of activity or experience that is divorced from culture or society. Rather, religion is pervasively present and is in complex interrelationships with all aspects of the peoples' life-ways. The chapters of this book provide examples of the manner in which religious elements are integrated into, and give definition to, specific cultural expressions of the arts and crafts, music, subsistence activities, and social and political organizations. Necessarily each chapter focuses upon specific examples of this integration of religion, or the sacred, with daily life in the context of a particular tribal group.

In spite of the rich diversity of formal expressions in widely disparate cultures, all the chapters define a range of fundamental principles which is central to and operative within any one Native American culture. These shared principles underlie sacred concepts that are specific to each of nature's manifestations and also to what could be called sacred geography. There obtains, in addition, a special understanding of language in which words constitute distinct units of sacred power, just as in the visual arts the depicted form *is* what it represents. Such concepts of sacred forms extend to diverse architectural styles, so that each dwelling, no matter how simple, is an image of the cosmos. Dimensions of the sacred are made specific in every situation and are intensified through an enormous variety of special rites and ceremonies which embrace each person's life and the totality of *all* life. These fundamental principles, expressed in different cultural contexts through differing formal expressions, not only provide a thread of unity throughout the book, but collectively also represent a model of the multiple dimensions of the sacred which come together in an organic interrelated manner in any one Native American culture. I have attempted to arrange the chapters in a sequence that would progressively spell out and clarify these core sacred qualities.

The first introductory chapter attempts to outline and situate geographically diverse Native American cultures, languages, and religious traditions. It is evident that in the Americas generally, and in North America specifically, there is neither *an* American Indian tradition nor *a* spiritual legacy, but rather a rich variety of both. To ignore such diversity of origin, place, language, and resulting cultural forms, as is so often done under a plethora of stereotypes, is to do great disservice to the American Indian peoples and their history. Throughout this opening chapter particular emphasis is placed on the also forgotten reality that these are religious traditions which, for many if not most of the peoples concerned, are living realities. Indeed, the contemporary and presiding emphasis among the peoples is upon both the restoration or revitalization of traditions which may have become neglected or forgotten, and their taking educational systems into their own hands in order to meet their particular cultural needs.

The second chapter presents a sampling of religious themes drawn essentially from the Plains Indians. The third chapter emphasizes the contemporary mood for the renewal of traditional practices within the larger secular world. Chapter four documents with specific examples the amazing persistence of essential values within today's world of accelerating change. Chapter five documents a presiding and central theme of probably all Native American life-ways and religious traditions which stands in contrast to most Western religions and experience, since these tend to dichotomize, to emphasize, as in this case, an opposition between the domains of contemplation and action. By contrast, in the Native American world there generally obtains what may be called a unity in experience wherein actions of all orders serve as supports for contemplation, for the sacred is understood to be mysteriously present within all forms of the phenomenal world as well as within all modes of action. It is perhaps this most important non-dualistic mode of experiencing and being that is very difficult for the non-Indian Western mind to comprehend. Chapter six spells out in greater detail this general theme of unity in experience, but in this case emphasizes the immediacy of the message of myths, heightened through timing, staging, and the total dynamic process of mythic narration.

Chapter seven is a poetic statement about the Sun Dance that attempts to capture some of the dignity, beauty, and profound heroic nature of this paramount ritual complex among the Plains Indians. The chapter following on mysticism stresses that among Native American peoples "mysticism" is not the vague "ism" as has so often become the case in certain Western contexts, but is rather a quality of spiritual participation which is framed and thus controlled by a range of specific rites involving the sacred forms of art, song, and dance. The rites and ceremonies of the Sun Dance itself, or the ritualized supports and requirements of the vision quest, are examples of frameworks through which sacred experiences are received and given direction in the life of the recipient. Chapter nine outlines the implications of the dominant contemporary concepts of linear and segmented time as contrasted with the rhythmical and cyclical concepts of time that are universally held in the original traditions of Native American peoples. The concluding chapter summarizes many of the values presented in preceding chapters, but with emphasis here upon the spiritual quality of the person which participation in such values and realities tend to form.

"We are all related" is a statement of profound implication made by each Lakota after he or she has smoked a sacred pipe in common and in communion. It is hoped that something of this quality of relationship is sensed throughout this book.

JOSEPH EPES BROWN

INTRODUCTION

It is no exaggeration to say that the publication of Joseph Epes Brown's first book, *The Sacred Pipe*, reignited interest in Native American religious traditions.[1] Immediately after the Second World War, this interest was at a low ebb. The last fighting Native American generation was about to disappear, and with them the old societies and their traditions. Anthropologists were concerned with White-Indian acculturation, since it was taken for granted that Native American cultures were going to be absorbed by white urban civilization. At that time, religion was of no major concern in anthropological development. Only a few scholars, like Ruth Underhill, Robert Lowie, and Paul Radin, still kept the scholarly interest in Native American religious traditions alive. What otherwise remained was the popular interest in Native American history, including old rituals.

During his student years, Joseph Brown himself experienced the despiritualization of Native American cultural studies. I remember how he once criticized one of his anthropological professors, the famous Dr. Leslie Spier, for his quantitative analysis of religious ceremonies such as the Sun Dance.[2] Joseph Brown's criticism did not attack the fact that Spier and other anthropologists had placed religion among other cultural phenomena. Joseph Brown pointed out that religion cannot be separated from any aspects of culture, and informed his readers that no Native American language has a word for religion. "It is thus preferable to use a term such as 'traditions' . . . when referring to religion among American Indians."[3]

---

[1] Joseph Epes Brown, *The Sacred Pipe: Black Elk's Account of the Seven Rites of the Oglala Sioux* (Norman, OK: University of Oklahoma, 1953).

[2] See Leslie Spier, "The Sun Dance of the Plains Indians: Its Development and Diffusion," *Anthropological Papers of the American Museum of Natural History*, vol. XVI:7 (New York, 1921).

[3] Joseph Epes Brown, "Religions in Primal Societies: North American Indian Religions," in *A Handbook of Living Religions*, ed. by John R. Hinnells (Harmondsworth: Penguin Books, 1984), p. 394. See also Joseph Epes Brown, *The Spiritual Legacy of the American Indian: Commemorative Edition with Letters While Living with Black Elk* (Bloomington, IN: World Wisdom, Inc., 2007), p. 2. Cf. my own position in Hultkrantz, "The Notion of Religion in the Research on North American Indian Religions," in *The Notion of "Religion" in Comparative Research*, ed. by Ugo Bianchi (Rome: "L'Erma" di Bretschneider, 1994), pp. 207-213.

What Joseph Brown was criticizing was a viewpoint and a methodology that ignores empathy for religion, or religious tradition. He held that religion has to be experienced just as the Native Americans themselves formulate it. The penetrating observer feels at one with the Native American, accepts—momentarily at least—his or her beliefs and perceptions. One can feel this on the vision quest, or at ritual situations such as the Sun Dance. I myself attended a Spirit Lodge ceremony in which, under the darkness of the Lodge, the medicine man's blanket was thrown over the body of a white observer who admitted afterwards that she did not believe in the message of the ceremony. As Joseph Brown recognized, the role of the "participating observer" requires that one not only follows the outer forms of a ceremony, but also accepts its premises. This is the hardest challenge for an anthropologist or a student of religion.

Is then such an attitude acceptable in the comparative study of religion which demands an open investigation of all religions? There are different solutions to this issue. Joseph Brown himself believed that all religions are expressions of the same wisdom. He cultivated this belief through his association with the *philosophia perennis* movement introduced by René Guénon and continued by Frithjof Schuon and Titus Burckhardt. Behind the *philosophia perennis* approach lies the search for a common factor inspiring all religions, or, as Schuon described it, the "transcendent unity of the religions." Joseph Brown's agreement with the *philosophia perennis* movement is important to keep in mind when reading his publications. At the same time, it is necessary to point out that his ideological commitments do not invalidate his empirical writings. Rather, they appear in his long range speculation of values, for instance, in an article he wrote more than thirty years ago, "The Spiritual Legacy of the American Indian."[4] Here he states that Native American human and spiritual resources have been "consciously and actively destroyed by a civilization which is out of balance precisely because it has lost those values" by which the American Indian lived.[5]

At the end of the article, the author identifies three stages of spiritual progress among Native Americans: purification, expansion, and union with Truth (or God). He finds this pattern recurring in all the great religions of the world, and also recognizes it among the Plains

---

[4] It certainly is no coincidence that this article was later incorporated into the first edition of this book. The title presents its author's message in a nutshell.

[5] Joseph Epes Brown, *The Spiritual Legacy of the American Indian*, p. 21.

Indians.[6] "If we can understand . . . the truths which the Indian finds in his relationships to nature, and the profound values reflected by his many rites and symbols, then we may become enriched, our understanding will deepen, and we shall be able to give to the American Indian heritage its rightful place among the great spiritual traditions of mankind."[7]

These beautiful words communicate the ideas of the *philosophia perennis*, and who could object to them? Joseph Brown has expressed his own conviction, just as other authors do when they explore the mysteries and rituals Native Americans experience. Why should the agnostic pronouncements be considered more accurate than the more positive reactions? Joseph Brown's evaluations constitute the ideological frame of facts which are reliable and which, I may add, reveal religious details that many other field workers have ignored.

This is what made Joseph Brown's approach to Native American religious traditions so exciting when it was first presented in *The Sacred Pipe*. Here he conveyed Black Elk's instruction to his people about the Oglala's most important rituals. With characteristic humility, Joseph Brown did not show himself as the creator of the book. He called himself the recorder and editor, and the dedication of the book is in Black Elk's words, "To my people the Sioux." It was Joseph Brown's first book, and it was received with acclaim by Native Americans and Non-Natives all over the world. Although Native Americans usually react negatively to the recounting of their rituals, this book has been welcomed and has served as a model of tribal life. Some fifteen years ago, I witnessed a ceremony arranged by Joseph Brown in which several stately Sioux chiefs received the book from his own hands. The Native Americans were solemn and appreciative. Native Americans often consider books written about them by Whites to be unreliable, but here was an author who had received his authority from one of their own great men.

The scholarly world also praised Joseph Brown's and Black Elk's book. A reviewer in *The American Anthropologist* wrote, "Ritual literature is often dull reading, but Brown's prose is free of archaism and

---

[6] Joseph Epes Brown, "The Spiritual Legacy" (1964), pp. 26 f. This pattern is of course the well-known contemplative scale of the mystics, *via purgativa*, *via illuminativa*, and *via unitiva*. Brown refers here to the visionary quest so common among North American Indians. See Joseph Epes Brown, *Animals of the Soul: Sacred Animals of the Oglala Sioux* (Rockport, MA: Element, 1992), pp. xi f. A good description of this rite is contained in *The Sacred Pipe*, pp. 44-66.

[7] Joseph Epes Brown, "The Spiritual Legacy" (1964), p. 27.

pedantry, and conveys a quality of the deepest sincerity."[8] *The Sacred Pipe* has been translated into more languages than any other book on Native Americans. It is indeed the book of introduction to North American Indian traditions almost everywhere, and is discussed and quoted by scholars and amateurs alike. Its popularity is unparalleled.

From the platform of the Plains Indians, Joseph Brown gained a perspective from which he could survey the total field of North American Indian religious traditions. Though he focuses on many specific tribes and cultural areas, the central theme of his approach is the wholeness that unites all Native Americans in a common view of life and ideas. Joseph Brown developed this thesis in a series of papers, many of which have been printed in this book. Its aim is to reevaluate still existing Native American primal traditions, and to free them from outmoded prejudices. His holistic perspective does not cause him to neglect the complicated tissue of cultural and religious threads. On the contrary, the author pays close attention to the various traditional expressions in different areas; he even talks of "North American Indian Living Religions."[9] Yet he finds similar principles behind the varied religious expressions. For instance, the structures of most Native American houses, whether they are Delaware long houses or Kiowa tipis, reiterate the cosmological values of the Universe.

Joseph Brown's view of Native American religious traditions has a firm and consequent structure. An important element is his conviction that all so-called new religions in modern times, such as the Peyote religion, are not innovations, but new variations of traditional religion. Even the teachings of the missionaries were accepted on these grounds: "the people easily understood the truths of message and example due to the profundity of their own beliefs; it was not difficult for them to adopt and adapt new expressions of values into the sacred fabric of their own religious culture." This can be seen in Black Elk's own experience as a catechist. As DeMallie put it, Black Elk "could express his firm belief in the truth of the Catholic religion without the necessity of rejecting Indian beliefs."[10] The same scholar has also noted that, as Brown's book shows, Black Elk structured Lakota rituals in a parallel

---

[8] Reviewed by Gordon W. Hewes in *The American Anthropologist* 56 (5), 1954, p. 909.

[9] Joseph Epes Brown, *The Spiritual Legacy of the American Indian*, pp. 1-20.

[10] Raymond J. DeMallie, ed., *The Sixth Grandfather* (Lincoln, NE: University of Nebraska, 1984), p. 66.

fashion to the Catholic sacraments.[11] In their general outlook on religion, Joseph Brown and Black Elk were twin souls.

Another interesting point in Joseph Brown's authorship is his emphasis on Native American consciousness of the relations of all beings, once more an expression of the holistic interpretation of religion. Other authors have also suggested the same thing, for instance, Irving Hallowell.[12] Joseph Brown, however, has spoken of this interrelatedness more persistently than anybody else. These thoughts underlie much of what has been said in *The Sacred Pipe* and *Animals of the Soul.* Repeatedly, the words of Black Elk are pronounced, "We are all related."[13] In this book, *The Spiritual Legacy of the American Indian*, Brown has given a very precise description of how this interrelatedness works. He points out how, unlike Western categories, Native American traditions refrain from fragmenting human experience into dichotomies. Native Americans tend "to stress modes of interrelatedness across categories of meaning, never losing sight of an ultimate wholeness." They discard, for instance, the animate-inanimate dichotomy; even rocks may have a life of their own.[14]

In conformity with this understanding, Joseph Brown realizes that most Native American tribes erase the walls between humans and animals. If there are perceived differences, the animal beings are seen by the Native Americans as superior (see the mythologies where the first beings are portrayed as some kind of prototypes of present-day animals). Among the Pawnee, the council of animals sends some of their members to help out human individuals who are in trouble.[15] All this is no doubt correct. At the same time, I think we must realize that it is humankind, not the animals, that is the great focus of human interest. No wonder, therefore, that in many Native American psychologies,

---

[11] Raymond J. DeMallie, ed., *The Sixth Grandfather*, p. 71.

[12] A. Irving Hallowell, "Ojibwa Ontology, Behavior, and World View," in *Culture in History*, ed. by Stanley Diamond (New York: Columbia University Press, 1960), pp. 19-64.

[13] Joseph Epes Brown, *The Sacred Pipe*, particularly p. 15 n. 5.

[14] Joseph Epes Brown, *The Spiritual Legacy of the American Indian*, p. 54. Quite a different thing is the fact that we find a mythological and sociological dualism in the organization of many tribes, and there are many dualistic myths. But this is not what the author refers to in his demonstration of "ultimate wholeness."

[15] Joseph Epes Brown, *The Spiritual Legacy of the American Indian*, p. 94.

only humans are equipped with a full scale of souls. More remarkable animals may have a complete set, for instance, the bear, but this is more rare.[16]

Joseph Brown explores other "spiritual legacies" that the Native American traditions have preserved, such as the nature of symbolism and the sacred. He points out that our concept of symbol as a substitute for the real thing is at odds with Native American belief. For Native Americans, the symbol *is*, in a sense, that to which it refers; the meaning is grasped intuitively.[17] I agree in principle, but I believe the problem is more intricate than that. When Joseph Brown assures us that in Native American traditions, the Sun is not God, but God manifested in the Sun—and I think he is referring to the Oglala of his field research—this is more than a case of symbolism. It is information concerning the distributive power of the Supreme Being into lesser divinities, as told to us by Walker and Densmore.[18] On the other hand, when a Catholic prays to Christ through his crucifix and experiences how the picture of Christ becomes Christ, a divinity who moves his eyes and sheds tears, has not this symbol become that to which it refers? Apparently, the Native American understanding of symbolism is not so unique, and Joseph Brown agrees with that.[19]

Joseph and I have discussed the concept of the "sacred," and though we have arrived at different conclusions, we both admit that the question is complex and difficult.[20] It would scarcely be suitable to discuss it more exhaustively here, but some points could be mentioned. For Joseph Brown, the sacred was a pervasive quality among

[16] Cf. Åke Hultkrantz, *Conceptions of the Soul among North American Indians,* Statens Ethnografiska Museum, Monograph Series No. 1, Stockholm 1953, pp. 483-497, p. 510.

[17] Joseph Epes Brown, *The Spiritual Legacy of the American Indian,* p. 55.

[18] On this problem, see Hultkrantz, *Belief and Worship in Native North America* (Syracuse, NY: Syracuse University Press, 1981), and Joseph Epes Brown, *The Spiritual Legacy of the American Indian* pp. 53-54.

[19] Joseph Epes Brown, *The Spiritual Legacy of the American Indian,* p. 55 f.

[20] In *The Sacred Pipe,* p. 3 n. 1, Joseph Brown translates Lakota *wakan* as "holy" or "sacred" although, as he informs us, it may also be rendered as "power, powerful." Other Plains Indians, such as the Shoshoni, have different words for sacred (supernatural) and power, cf. Hultkrantz, "The Meaning of Terms for the Supernatural in Shoshoni Indian Religion," in *Tradition and Translation,* ed. by Christopher Elsas, et al., (Berlin and New York: Walter de Gruyter, 1994).

Native Americans: "the sacred is understood to be mysteriously present within all forms of the phenomenal world as well as within all modes of action."[21] "The total world of experience is seen as being infused with the sacred."[22] Here, as so many times before, Joseph Brown avoids dichotomization and spells out the unity of the experiences as the dominant feature.

Joseph Brown certainly had reasons to postulate a Native American belief in the unity of the sacred. Black Elk talks about the sacred pipe, the sacred earth, the sacred day, the sacred bundle, the sacred place, the sacred corn, and so on. However, I do not find one statement in the book implying that the human beings are sacred as such. Only from an inference from the following Black Elk quote could this conclusion be vaguely drawn: "We should understand well that all things are the works of the Great Spirit. We should know that He is within all things: the trees, the grasses, the rivers, the mountains, and all the four-legged animals, and the winged people; and even more important, we should understand that He is also above all things and people."[23] We notice that the human beings are not included in this enumeration. There is also no hint that all these everyday phenomena are sacred as such.

In my opinion, Black Elk's enumeration of sacred objects prevents us from applying the interpretation that everything is considered sacred. If the latter were the case, why then point out particular phenomena as sacred? How could you have sacred places and days if all places and days are sacred? There are, however, some circumstances that make my conclusion uncertain. It is possible I have missed pronouncements by Black Elk that point in another direction. Moreover, Joseph Brown lived with Black Elk and his family for a long time, and he could have grasped intuitively Black Elk's intentions—and we all know what a good religious intuition Joseph Brown possessed. Finally, perhaps nothing certain can be said about the general Lakota understanding until the statements of other Oglala authorities have been examined.

[21] Joseph Epes Brown, *The Spiritual Legacy of the American Indian*, p. xv.

[22] Joseph Epes Brown, *The Spiritual Legacy of the American Indian*, p. 56. Cf. also Joseph Brown's letter in Michael O. Fitzgerald, *Yellowtail: Crow Medicine Man and Sun Dance Chief* (Norman, OK: University of Oklahoma, 1991), p. 213.

[23] Joseph Epes Brown, *The Sacred Pipe*, p. xx.

The following ritual memory from a spring day in 1980 still enchants me: Joseph had driven me to a sacred yellow pine tree close to the southern end of the Bitterroot Valley. The pine is known as the Bighorn Tree. The horns of a bighorn ram are deeply embedded inside it as a result of a fight between coyote and a bighorn sheep in past time. Offerings to the tree are said to give luck. At our visit, Joseph produced some light tobacco pouches, attached some feathers and glass beads to them and then silently walked around the tree. At each of the four cardinal points, he turned towards the tree, lifted a pouch, and looked at the sky. He then placed the offered pouch at the base of the tree trunk. This was truly an act of ritual participation in Native American religious tradition. To Joseph Epes Brown, it was also an act of *religio perennis*.

ÅKE HULTKRANTZ

CHAPTER 1

NORTH AMERICAN INDIAN
LIVING RELIGIONS

The following treatment of elements of American Indian living religions must be both cursory and selective. Even where emphasis is to
be upon the present living reality and viability of religious elements,
account must be taken of at least the following three major interrelated factors.

First, American Indian religions represent preeminent examples of
primal religious traditions that have been present in the Americas for
some thirty to sixty thousand years. Fundamental elements common
to the primal nature of those traditions not only survive into the present among Indian cultures of the Americas, but in many cases are currently being reexamined and reaffirmed by the people with increasing
and remarkable vigor.

Second, out of this heritage of primal qualities there has developed, through time and in accord with the great geographical diversity
of the Americas, a rich plurality of highly differentiated types of religious traditions, making it impossible to define or describe American
Indian religions in generalities.

Third, ever-increasing contacts since the late fifteenth century
with representatives of diverse civilizations and cultures of Europe and
Euro-Americans led to a vast spectrum of change within and across
indigenous Indian cultures. Under this impact certain tribal groups and
even linguistic families became extinct, while others became accultur-
ated to varying degrees into the dominant societies.

Most surviving groups, however, have shown through history a
remarkable ability for coping with change and cultural deprivation by
adapting and borrowing from the non-Indian world with pragmatic yet
cautious selectivity, making it possible not just to survive but to retain
at least core elements of ancient and well-tried religions and traditional
ways of being. The "new" religious movements of revitalization or
reformulation, in response to deprivation and continuing pressures for
acculturation, should therefore be understood in terms of a continuity of traditional elements rather than as innovations unrelated to the

peoples' own religious and cultural history. The impact of Christianity and the special meaning of "conversion" to the American Indian should also be understood in this larger context.

THE PRIMAL FOUNDATIONS

Those primal elements that are universal and fundamental to virtually all North American Indian religious traditions of past or present include the following general qualities or traits.

1. That which we refer to in current usage as "religion" cannot be conceived as being separable from any of the multiple aspects of any American Indian culture. In no American Indian language is there any single word or term that could translate as "religion," as there is no single term for what we refer to as "art." To stress this distinctive phenomenon it is preferable to use a term such as "traditions," or perhaps, for greater clarity, "religious traditions," when referring to religion among American Indians or indeed among any primal peoples.

2. Within primal or "primitive" cultures the people's understanding of their language involves at least the following elements. Words have a special potency or force that is integral to their specific sounds: What is named is therefore understood to be really present in the name in unitary manner, not as "symbol" with dualistic implication, as is generally the case with modern languages. An aspect of the sacred potency latent in words in primal tradition is the presiding understanding that words in their sounds are born in the breath of the being from whom they proceed, and since breath in these traditions is universally identified with the life principle, words are thus sacred and must be used with care and responsibility. Such quality of the spoken word is further enhanced by the understood close proximity of the source of breath, the lungs, with the heart, which is associated with the being's spiritual center.

Just as words bear power, the full statement, or even an unspoken thought, is understood to have a compulsive potency of its own, especially when the utterance is in a ritual or ceremonial context. Recitation of a myth of creation, for example, is understood to be an actual, not a symbolic, recapitulation or reenactment of that primordial creative process or event, which is not bound by time.[1]

---

[1] Perhaps the most attention that has been given to these primal qualities of language, including that equally or more important paralanguage of silence, is in the studies of Dennis and Barbara Tedlock (see chapter 10, footnote 2), who have drawn their examples primarily from the Zunis of the American Southwest.

3. A similar mode of understanding, paralleling that of language, is found in the way American Indian peoples perceive what we call their arts and crafts. The natural materials used in the creative activity manifest sacred powers in accord with their particular nature and place of origin; and the completed form itself, or what is externally "represented," is seen to manifest its own sacred potency, but again, not in the dual manner or process by which we translate a "symbol." Such immediate quality of experience is essential to an outsider's understanding of the rich legacy of American Indian art forms, and is also a key to the realization that here there can be no sharp dichotomy as obtains between our categories of the "arts" as distinct from the "crafts."

4. Further primal concepts pervasive and basic to American Indian traditions are found in the experience of time and process, which are universally understood not in the Western linear manner, but in terms of the circle—that is, cyclical and reciprocal. The seasons of nature, the span of a life, human or non-human, are understood in a cyclical manner and are reexpressed formally in architectural styles reflecting the cosmos and through a rich variety of ritual or ceremonial forms and acts.

5. A presiding characteristic of primal people is a special quality and intensity of interrelationship with the forms and forces of their natural environment. As nomadic hunters or gatherers, or as agriculturists, dependence upon natural resources demanded detailed knowledge of all aspects of their immediate habitat. This accumulated pragmatic lore was, however, always interrelated with a sacred lore; together these could be said to constitute a metaphysic of nature. It is therefore possible to speak of subsistence activities in terms of sacred modes of hunting and fishing, or to define in great detail rich cosmological lore latent in agricultural pursuits. American Indian peoples are today giving new attention to the wisdom of these traditions, and such reevaluation is having a strong impact upon certain non-Indian groups who are concerned with environmental degradation within the industrialized societies.

Out of the foundations of these still-lived primal elements, there developed in the Americas through time and across space specific traditions of great diversity. The migrations over successive time periods, the diversity of physical types, a thousand or more tribal groups with several hundred mutually unintelligible languages for North America alone, and all with the contrasts of American geography and climatic zones to which the peoples adapted, present complexities and questions that still evade scholars. Full descriptions and formulations of typologies within the subtle and sensitive area of native religious traditions is a work still to be accomplished, and is further complicated by historical overlays of Euro-American presences and their introduction, with proselytizing zeal and quasi-divine mandate, of new religio-cultural elements. The appended map of "culture areas" (see p. 98) will express and perhaps clarify some elements of this grand complexity.

In response to increasing evidence of this cultural plurality, the concept of Native American "culture areas" was conceived and developed at the turn of the century by Clark Wissler. This is a concept that necessarily oversimplifies and raises problems, such as its static perspective and the cultural identity of people where areas converge and overlap. Yet the device is deemed useful here as a means for organizing descriptive materials and for employing certain generalizations within circumscribed limits. The five culture areas that have been selected for summary description both represent a cross-section of North American indigenous peoples and provide examples of religious traditions as related to contrasting subsistence patterns.

The general primal qualities already outlined, with the more specific traits to be described, may be said to constitute *living* religions in the sense that core elements of sacred lore, values, and the native language are held and lived today by at least certain segments of the populations, and it is through the leaders of these groups that movements for preservation and revitalization are appearing with increasing frequency. Analysis of the impact and meaning of Christianity and conversion among American Indian groups will be presented in the concluding part of this chapter.

THE ARCTIC ESKIMO

The Eskimo of the arctic coast, whose religious traits are representative of a larger circumpolar region, are often excluded from descriptions of the more southern Indians. Such exclusion is arbitrary, since evidence suggests that many core arctic and closely related subarctic religious themes diffused southward, where, with certain modifications and additions, they survive today in the lives of eastern woodland Algonquin hunting peoples, among the Athabascans of the western subarctic, and even among the peoples of the Plains and Prairie cultural area.

The Eskimo experience their world of barren coast and expanse of sea and ice as peopled with a vast host of spirit beings whose differentiated qualities and associated powers are specific to each form and force of the natural environment. There are also spirits, no less real, which are of realms unrelated to forms of the phenomenal world. Graphic depiction of such spirit realities is expressed by the people in abundance, as executed in the ancient tradition of stone carvings or through contemporary innovative lithographs, as produced, for example, by the peoples of the Cape Dorset Cooperatives. Precarious subsistence dependency upon sea mammals, or land animals in season, is interrelated with beliefs in a soul or plurality of souls specific to all human and nonhuman living beings. In slaying animals of the sea or land, the hunter thus bears grave responsibility for releasing souls (*anua*) of living beings; rites and ceremonies must therefore be observed in relation to all aspects of hunting. The Eskimo indeed hold that the greatest danger in their lives is not the cold or constant threat of starvation, but the presiding reality that their existence is dependent upon the taking of life from other beings. In a world where such precarious balance obtains between life and death, or where such a thin line divides physical appearances from the subtle realm of spirits, it is understandable that there must be specific structures and mechanisms by which equilibrium can be maintained.

Equilibrium within families and larger social groups depends upon observing a host of taboos specific to every necessary activity and social interrelationship. Where codes of such appropriate behavior are broken, or where the attitudes of the hunter are not respectful toward the game, it is believed that the animals will not present themselves willingly as a sacrificial offering to the hunter.

These traditions of the coastal arctic peoples are expressed and supported by beliefs in an all-powerful goddess, half human and half fish, called Sedna or Takanaluk, who dwells in a great cave or pool under the sea wherein she keeps all the sea mammals, which she will release or withhold according to the degree to which the people observe or break the taboos. In parallel manner, there are Masters or Keepers of the various species of land animals, who will release or withhold their kind according to the behavior and attitudes of the hunter and the hunter's people. These beliefs suggest the presence of an abstract and unifying concept, since the multiplicity of spirits and souls of all sea life coalesce into a kind of unity in the single underwater Sea Power, as in similar manner the spirits of land animals are unified under the single great Master or Keeper. Although it is not possible to affirm for the Eskimo an even more ultimate concept of a High God responsible for all life, as is found in most Indian tribes to the south, there nevertheless is occasional reference to a unity of all living beings of sea and land in the figure of the Great Meat Dish. If such seemingly more ultimate and unitary concept may not be central to Eskimo experience, it could well be due to the fact that human survival here necessitates presiding attention to the immediate and specific elements of a harsh and precarious environment.

In this arctic world of uncertainties, the central and all-important religious practitioner is the *angákut*, or shaman, which is the customary Siberian Tungusic term. This shaman helps the people maintain the necessary delicate balance between this world of pragmatic necessities and the more subtle, but no less real world of spirits, souls, and gradated powers. The shaman is an intermediary between these multiple worlds, who can communicate, interpret, and indeed travel in mysterious flight through the worlds of Eskimo realities. The shaman's wisdom and special powers are critical to communal life and human survival. Through the shaman's familiarity with the spirit realms and through his ability to send out in ecstatic trance one of his souls, often called the "free soul," on a spiritual journey and quest, he is able to discern who among the people has broken the taboos causing the disappearance of the game. He is able to placate Sedna under the sea, or discover the cause of illness perhaps associated with "soul loss," or he may foretell future weather conditions and thus the appropriate time for travel.

Methods of becoming a shaman are common to many Indian groups of the Americas. The apprentice must have a guide who has traveled and knows the way. Among many disciplines, he must learn from his instructor how to divest himself, in sacred and mysterious manner, of the outer layers of his own flesh, and then to name all the bones of his skeleton. In such magical lore is clarified the deep meanings underlying widespread traditions of shamanic art forms found throughout the arctic and Indian Americas, wherein the outer covering of beings is understood and presented as transparent, a kind of x-ray vision that focuses on depicted inner or vital realities understood in a spiritual manner. To gain the shamanic lore, the apprentice must also participate in a retreat where, through the secrets of solitude and in suffering through fasting and exposure to cold, he will receive, if he is worthy, specific sacred powers through the vision appearance and the teachings of a helping spirit.

The novice shaman must then observe special taboos and requirements when he returns to his people, whom he is now able to lead through the delicate balance of life and death as an intermediary for the subtle forces of the spirit worlds. Demonstration of the powers received is required in periodic communal gatherings where, with the aid of the powerful rhythms of drum and voice, and with a rich array of dramatic props and techniques, the shaman enters into ecstatic trance, during which his soul travels to find and return with the needed knowledge. His success or failure as a shaman is established for the people in accord with the pragmatic or spiritual results obtained. Such practices and shamanic lore confirm for the people the realities of the worlds of spirits and souls, afford release from personal and communal tensions, and define order and structures critical to stability and continuity of the family and larger society in a harsh and precarious environment.

THE EASTERN SUBARCTIC

Religious elements central to the arctic peoples are recapitulated, with certain variations and additions, in the lives of the northern Algonquin hunters who adapted to conditions of the boreal regions of the subarctic. In spite of changes wrought by a long history of contact with Euro-American hunters, trappers, traders, and Christian missionaries, the hunting activities of these people are still imbued with sacred beliefs and accompanying rites similar in most respects to those of the arctic. Here, however, are found rich mythologies of creation with an anthropomorphic Creator figure who is found upon the primordial waters, accompanied by already present aquatic diving birds and animals, and who brings to the surface of the waters the primal mud from which the earth is fashioned. This mythic theme instructs, among many other things, that creation is not just an event of time past but is an ever-continuing process in which all elements of creation participate now as always.

Also, there are tales of ambivalent Trickster hero figures who bring desirable things to the people while defining through their unacceptable acts the parameters of acceptable behavior. The conical-frame wigwam type of dwelling is conceived by the people as a recreated image of the cosmos, or of the human being as a microcosm, as is also reflected in the dome-shaped "sweat lodge." In such lodges the regenerative forces of earth, air, fire, and water are used in combination for restoring a man's original purity, which may be lost through the breaking of innumerable hunting taboos or through contact with the ritual impurity associated with the menstrual cycles of women. The smoking pipes and tobacco used in this area carry eminently sacred and sacramental meanings. Although it is true that tobacco smoking is found on the arctic coast, evidence suggests that its origin is from the west, from

Russia through Siberia, which explains the absence of sacred elements associated with smoking among the Eskimo.

The religious practitioners of the western and eastern subarctic represent a modification of the classic shamanism of the arctic and Siberia, for here the shaman does not send out in ecstatic trance one of his souls to accomplish a mission; rather, in dramatic ceremony within the lodge, and with the use of the drum and offerings, he conjures *in* to himself his spirit helpers, whom he had experienced in the course of a vision quest. These spirits demonstrate their presence by mysteriously tapping and shaking the lodge, at times accompanied by mysterious sounds. The spirits, who are sometimes the practitioner's guardian spirits, are then instructed to seek out and bring back what is desired of them.

As is appropriate to a people whose lives are dependent upon the hunting and trapping of large and small game, there obtains rich and sacred lore relating to all the animals in their world of experience. Special qualities are specific to each species of animal, and these qualities can be communicated to the people. Animals are thus considered as teachers and, in a sense, are therefore superior to humans. Due to such beliefs the people have secret societies of animal lodges, which often are ranked in accordance with the powers specific to the particular animal. The bear, for example, is considered to be of the greatest power, thus complex rites and ceremonies are found in the hunting, slaying, and final sacramental treatment of this animal, especially concerning the appropriate and respectful disposal of the bones and skull. The key Algonquin term that refers to sacred power as used here is *manitu*, with *Kitchi Manitou* being the totality of all such powers. It is suggested by certain scholars that the latter term, which suggests an overall unitary principle, originated with the coming of Christianity; yet it is also highly probable, as much evidence suggests, that this concept was understood prior to the advent of Euro-Americans.

THE EASTERN WOODLANDS

Moving southward from the coastal arctic to the subarctic and into the eastern woodlands, there is a cumulative continuity of core religious themes, their ritual and ceremonial expressions increasingly complex as climate and habitat become more favorable. Such complexity is well illustrated by the Medewewin medicine dance, or the Medicine Lodge Society of the Ojibwa-Chippewa of the Great Lakes region. These ceremonies normally occur semi-annually in late spring and early fall. Candidates seek initiation into the sacred society for a variety of reasons, but most often they have had dream or vision experiences in retreats that indicate they should seek admission. Such persons are then instructed by the *mide* priests in the sacred lore, songs, and other requirements for entry.

The Medewewin rites are conducted within a long lodge conceived as an image of the universe. Purification in a sweat lodge is required prior to participation in the ceremonies. Within the lodge, and guarding the doorways, are certain forms identified with animal-spirit helpers and guardians. The rites may last from two to eight days, depending on the degrees the candidates are entering. The first of these cumulative degrees is associated with aquatic animals referred to in myths of creation: the mink, otter, muskrat, or beaver. The second degree is associated with the beings of the air, an owl or a hawk, and the third degree with more powerful beings of the earth such as the serpent or wildcat. The fourth and ultimate degree, which may be achieved in older age and which demands much time, preparation, and expense, is represented by the most powerful land animal, the bear. Within the lodge myths are recited by the priests or medicine men that tell of creation and sacred migration, such recitations usually supported by incised birch-bark scrolls, which act as a mnemonic aid. The ceremonies come to a dramatic climax when the candidates are ritually "shot" by the priests, using an otterskin bag out of which the sacred *mi'gis* or cowrie shell is magically propelled into the candidate, who drops to the ground experiencing a spiritual death. In being brought back to life by the priest, the candidate is understood to be reborn into a new world of deeper spiritual understanding.

Although these Algonquin peoples have had intense contacts over many centuries with Euro-American peoples and cultures, and have experienced loss of lands, new types of subsistence economies, the introduction of Christianity, and most recently the new syncretistic Peyote religion of the Native American Church, rites such as those of the Medewewin are not only still observed, but there is evidence of increasing participation. Such renewed affirmation of traditional religious elements may in part be explained by the new pan-Indian movements, which so facilitate intertribal exchange that other centers of traditional renewal, as found for example in the Plains, provide example and stimulus to tribal groups of distant areas.

The dominant Iroquoian-speaking peoples of a still more favorable eastern woodland environment represent even greater cultural complexity in their dual subsistence patterns of horticulture, probably of southeastern origin, and seasonal hunting. Their wise and well-known sociopolitical league organization of the six nations, although some-what changed and modified, is still intact and operative today in its basic structure, as is the case with many of the traditional Iroquoian religious expressions that endure beneath the obvious external evidence of change.

Iroquoian religion gives ultimate attention to a supreme and unitary principle which, although claimed by many to be of Christian origin, nevertheless seems to be integral from the earliest times to a host of core indigenous Iroquoian expressions and general world view. Their term *Orenda*, which defines an extension of spiritual power(s), is a concept which, although expressed in different languages, is widespread across American Indian cultures. Such an abstract concept is basic to Iroquoian cosmologies, which define dualisms of heaven and earth, but which understand them to be necessary reciprocal forces that are ultimately inherent in a unitary principle. The structure of the Iroquoian longhouses expresses these cosmological values, and it is in such houses that the people to this day enact cycles of complex four-day dance-drama ceremonies, often of thanksgiving, acknowledging and celebrating the gifts of life in the form of foods both wild and cultivated.

The Iroquoian carved masks of the False Face curing societies speak of the spirit forces of the woodlands, their powers intensified by the requirement that the marks be carved out of a standing living tree. The Iroquois have rites of purification, and youths are expected at puberty to engage in the vision quest, often to seek out a personal guardian spirit, which is usually associated with the person's new and sacred name. With the disruption of much of Iroquoian culture under an intensity of Euro-American contact and pressures for change, there appeared in the 1800s the Seneca prophet Handsome Lake, whom the people prefer to call the Life Bringer, who brought a messianic message with strict codes of conduct. As with the messianic movement of the 1890 Ghost Dance, or the Peyote cult that became incorporated as the Native American Church in 1918, the code of the Iroquois Life Bringer integrated traditional indigenous elements with selected Christian ethics and beliefs. It is in terms of such synthetic reformulations that members of the Iroquois league live their religions today.

THE PLAINS AND PRAIRIE

Native American groups living today in the Plains and Prairie area represent very diverse cultural histories, with tribal origins tracing back to the hunting cultures of the Athabascan Mackenzie subarctic, the eastern Algonquin woodlands, and the early agricultural traditions of the Southeast, as well as to certain groups of Uto-Aztecan gathering and hunting peoples from the Great Basin area. Given this great diversity of origins, languages, and cultures, it is difficult to understand in what sense this geographic zone may be said to constitute a single culture area with distinctive religious traditions. Yet over many centuries, with common adjustments to a unique Plains and Prairie grasslands environment supporting millions of bison, and with the advent of the horse in the 1800s leading to greater mobility and intensification of intertribal contacts, the diverse groups developed a style of life and thought expressing a commonality of religio-cultural traits. This cultural history presents a remarkable example of adaptability and selective borrowings that has continued into the present day even in confrontations with new elements and forces for change from Euro-American societies. It is this facility for adaptation that has allowed the people to survive with a distinctive Plains style and quality of core religious and ceremonial elements.

The Plains people define and experience a multitude of differentiated spirit beings or sacred powers, which (a) are specific to each form and element of the natural world; (b) are associated with vital force or an animating life principle; and (c) possess subtle qualities understood to be transferable to other beings or even to "inanimate" forms. It should be noted that in the people's experience no hard dichotomy obtains between the Western categories of "animate" and "inanimate," since to them all phenomena are animate in some manner. The sacred quality of powers is denoted by terms such as the Dakota *wakan*, which is not a noun with the implication of limit, but an adjective conveying a sense of mystery or the mysterious. This multiplicity of sacred mysteries tends to coalesce into an ultimate unity expressed through polysynthetic terms such as the Lakota *Wakan-Tanka*, "Great Mysterious," similar to *Wakonda* among the Omaha and Osage. The often-used translation "Great Spirit" employs a noun, and is undoubtedly the result of a Christian perspective that changes the original sense of the term.

Almost all Plains tribal groups stress the importance of individual participation in a ritualized "vision quest," or less frequently a quest to receive one's personal guardian spirit, both forms being accomplished in solitary retreat with fasting and sacrifice. Sacred powers appearing in such experiences are usually associated with animal beings or with other natural phenomena, and they may indicate the seeker's sacred name, may constitute the origin and validation of sacred songs and forms of art, or may be the origin of a new tribal rite or ceremony. The nature of the received vision often obligates the recipient to externalize the experience and thus to share the power with the larger community through use of art representations or an actual reenactment of the experience through new forms of dance-drama. The obligation for all individuals to participate in a vision quest is so pervasive that Robert Lowie was led to term the trait "democratized shamanism."

The classical dwelling of Plains peoples is the portable conical tipi, which expresses cosmological and metaphysical meanings and is therefore still used for ceremonial occasions or for general communal gatherings such as the summer "powwows." The shelter is understood as the universe, or microcosmically as a human person. The central open fire is the presence of the Great Mysterious, which is at the center of all existence, and the smoke hole at the top of the tipi is the place and path of liberation. Similar understandings are specific to the small dome-shaped sweat lodge wherein, as with the eastern subarctic peoples, purification rites are required as preparation for sacred ceremonies, or before any important undertaking. Even though today most Plains people live in permanent frame houses, the purification lodges are usually found nearby.

The Sun Dance, also called Medicine Dance or Thirst Lodge, is an annual springtime world- or self-renewal ceremony of great complexity, which today has been particularly instrumental in the preservation and revitalization of many traditional religious elements. The large, circular open frame lodge is ritually constructed in imitation of the world's creation, with the sacred cottonwood tree at the center as the axis linking sky and earth. Those who have previously made the vow participate in the sacrificial dance-fast in the lodge for three to four days, dancing all day and most of the night with the powerful support of large drums and heroic songs. They move from the circumference to the tree at the center and back again, always facing and concentrating upon the tree at the center, or upon one of the sacred objects attached to the tree—an eagle or bison head or skull. Some groups, such as the Lakota, periodically move within the lodge in such a manner that the dancers are always gazing toward the sun, which is associated with the source of life. Some dancers make specific vows to pierce the muscles of their chests. Into these cuts are attached thongs that have been tied to a high point in the tree, so that the dancer is now virtually tied to the center and must dance until the flesh breaks loose. Through the rigors and sacrificial elements of these rites the individual participants often receive powers through vision experiences, and the larger community gathered in support of the dancers participates in the sacred powers thus generated.

The sacred tobacco pipes of the Plains peoples express in comprehensive synthetic manner all that is most sacred to the people. Such pipes are used on all ritual and important occasions, and any agreement or relationship sealed with the smoking of a pipe is held inviolate. Such pipes have sacred origins defined in rich mythologies, and there are pervasive beliefs, held to this day, that if ever the pipes are no longer used or respected the people will lose their center and will cease to be a people. The pipes, which have long wooden stems and stone bowls, are understood to be an axis joining and defining a path between heaven and earth. Microcosmically the pipe is identified with human beings, the stem being the breath passage leading to the bowl, which is the spiritual center or heart. In solemn prayer, as each grain of carefully prepared tobacco is placed in the pipe, mention is made of some aspect of creation, so that when the bowl is full it contains the totality of time, space, and all of creation including humankind. When the fire consumes this consecrated tobacco with the aid of human breath, there is affirmed the absorption, or identity, of all creation with the fire, which is the presence of the ultimate Great Mysterious. Often, in concluding the rite the participants in the communal smoking recite, "We are all related." Today certain Christian priests, realizing the profound meanings of the pipe, are attempting to integrate the rites within the context of celebration of Holy Communion. On the other hand, many of the younger traditional Indians have ambivalent feelings about such practices.

Religious practitioners in the Plains are often termed "medicine men" or "medicine women," for they are the ones who know the lore of curative herbs, a knowledge partly transferred but validated and added to through sacred lore received in the vision quest. There are also those who have received especially sacred powers and helpers through vision or dream experiences and are thereby qualified to guide others in the means to seek experience of the sacred. Both functions are often possessed by one person.

This type of person and function is somewhat different from the classical arctic shaman, for here the practitioner does not send out his or her "free soul" in a trance state to accomplish missions, but rather in dramatic ceremony the spirit helpers are called in and then sent out to discover the cause of illness, to find lost objects, or to provide an answer to some spiritual question. The contemporary *Yuwipi* ceremonies, now very popular among the Sioux, provide good examples of such a type of practitioner and the use of what may be called ceremonial magic.

Purification rites, vision quests, Sun Dances, rituals of the pipe, and other ceremonies of a traditional nature are being increasingly practiced by Plains peoples today, with positions of leadership being assumed by younger tribal members. Affirmation of certain traditional values is also being expressed in new contexts and through such means as the summer "powwow" circuit, offering a type of nomadism with intertribal pan-Indian emphasis. Even the once militant American Indian Movement, which used religious themes to support protest activities, is now minimizing militant protest in favor of sincere relearning and reliving the traditional religious ways in which more ultimate and lasting answers to problems and questions of identity are found. Statistics are not available, but significant evidence from Plains areas strongly suggests that the once rapidly expanding ceremonial use of peyote in the syncretistic Native American Church is now being superseded by the more satisfying and lasting realities found in the roots of the people's own indigenous traditional lore, which, moreover, is carried by their own languages.

THE SOUTHWEST

Due to rich cultural and linguistic diversity the American southwest as a cultural area is so complex that it is only possible to treat here in summary manner two dominant groups, the Pueblos and Navajo, or *Dimwe* (the people), as they prefer to be called.

The roots of the sedentary Pueblo cultures in the southwest reach back to both the Paleo-Indian big game hunters of approximately 10,000 B.C. and to the expansive Desert Culture of ±3000 B.C. with its evidence of incipient agriculture. Since these ancient times, the peoples have developed rich and complex cultures identified with specific regions and experienced a number of migrations before being located at their present sites along the Rio Grande in the east and extending to the Arizona mesas of the Hopi in the west.

The very distinct Athabascan (*Na Diné*)-speaking Navajo appeared in the southwest as recently as A.D. 1200-1400, having migrated south from their homelands in the Yukon-Mackenzie subarctic area. In the interrelationships between the Navajo and Pueblo peoples, and in the encounter of both groups with the later Spanish and Euro-American domination, they have each been able to retain into the present day their own unique identities. Remarkable examples are here found not only of cultural persistence throughout adaptation and change, but also of the enduring viability of the Navajo, whose original population in 1868 was approximately eight thousand; fifty thousand in 1950; eighty-five thousand in 1961; and at least one hundred and seventy-five thousand at present.

The Pueblos

It could be assumed that the Pueblos, as sedentary agricultural village people, would be especially vulnerable to those successive outside pressures for change on the part of the Spanish explorers and military, the Christian missionaries, and the detraditionalizing policies of the American government agencies. And yet through time and bitter experience the communities learned the wisdom of appearing to acquiesce while holding in secret to their own traditional beliefs and sacred rites and ceremonies. The profound and all-encompassing nature of these traditions, borne by languages the oppressors did not understand, explains the remarkable continuity and viability of the Pueblo peoples into the present day.

Although each of the many Pueblo communities holds to its own distinctive ways of belief and action, it is nevertheless possible to suggest certain generalizations if the differences are understood to be dialects of a commonly shared cosmological and spiritual language. The Pueblo cosmos is defined through mythic narrations expressing a varying number of spheres pierced through by a hollow vertical axis. Among the Zuni these spheres are described as seven in number. Commencing with the realm of A'wonawil'ona, understood as a supreme life-giving bisexual power, other spheres are identified in turn with the Sun Father, who gives light and warmth, and the Moon Mother, who gives light at night, divides the year into months, and expresses the life cycle of living beings. The central terrestrial fourth realm is of the Earth Mother, the provider of all vegetation. The fifth subterrestrial realm is associated with the gods of war, the twin culture heroes, and the sacred Corn Mother. The gods of the sixth realm are represented by persons wearing masks (the *koko*), who appear in the seasonal dance-drama, and the seventh realm is identified with the zoic gods.

Mythic accounts of the coming into being of human persons and animals in the terrestrial realm commence with descriptions of a dark underworld, an eminently sacred realm of undeveloped possibility. In the process of emerging into the terrestrial realm, amorphous "human" beings are led by solar heroes and are also aided by animal beings who explore in turn each sphere to the four horizontal cardinal directions. The actual process of vertical emergence is aided by four types of sacred trees identified with each of the four directions and upon which the beings climb upward to emerge into this world of limit and hardness but illuminated by the light of the sun.

It is through the full context of these myths, periodically retold in dramatic manner, that everything of importance for the people of this present terrestrial realm is defined: the heavenly elements of sun and moon, the four directions of horizontal space with their specific colors and identifying mountain ranges, the meanings associated with categories of trees, and the rich lore specific to each of the animals and birds, which is central to the structure and values of the people's many secret societies.

The Pueblo cosmos may be defined in terms of the duality of sacred worlds below in distinction to the more profane world into which the peoples emerged—comparatively a realm of hardness, limit, and restricted possibility. Among the Tewa peoples this dualism is defined through terms such as *ochu* (green, unripe, eminently sacred) in distinction to *seht'a* (cooked, ripe, or hardened); social categories, with their supernatural or posthumous counterparts, are defined and supported by such formulations. Thus it is clear why the most sacred places within the Pueblos are the *kivas*, or underground ceremonial chambers, at the bottom of which is a hollow shaft, the *sipapu*, leading underground and understood to be the very place of emergence, the Center of centers, and the underworld connection to the shrines located in the sacred mountains of the four directions. Within these *kivas*, present in varying numbers within each Pueblo, preparations take place for ceremonial rites and the dance-dramas of the masked deities that are enacted in accord with a carefully observed ceremonial calendar based on the seasons marked by the dualities of summer and winter solstices. The strict observance of the ceremonial cycle is controlled by a priest of a specific clan, who observes the annual movements of the sun. Access to the underground *kiva* is through a vertical ladder, so that descent and ascent recapitulates for the person the mythic process of emergence; it is also the way of access back to the sacred realm. The dance-dramas, which are prepared by the men in the *kivas*, are enacted in the appropriate season in the open village plazas; this periodic return of the deities reestablishes contact with the realm of the sacred.

Without the seasonal enactment of these rites and ceremonies it is believed that recycling of the sacred world- and life-sustaining powers will cease, the world will die, and the people will be no more. The pervasive force of such ritually enacted beliefs inhibits acculturation into the non-Pueblo world of other and predominantly secular values. The comprehensive nature of beliefs integrated into the totality of life-ways makes unattractive and unnecessary the taking on of new religious elements or movements from the non-Pueblo outside world. The Native American Church and the multiple Christian denominations have therefore made little inroad into Pueblo life.

The Navajo

As northern intruders into a southwestern area of enormous cultural complexity, it is understandable that many threads of present-day Navajo culture represent a complex of elements borrowed from the Pueblos, the Spanish, the Spanish-Americans, and the ever-changing presence of the American non-Indian world. The impact of these influences is intensified by the structured presence of increasing numbers of Christian missions of all denominations, by the endless stream of "civilizing" educational policies and various agents of the U. S. government, and by new religious movements such as the Native American Church. Yet in spite of obvious changes within ancient Athabascan life-ways resulting from these contacts and pressures, studies such as that of Evan Vogt[2] suggest that these multiple innovative elements, with the exception of certain Pueblo traits, have not become fused in an integrative manner into Navajo culture and world view or compartmentalized—as was the Pueblo response to pressures for change—but have been sequentially *incorporated* around a central structural framework that was and remains to this day distinctly Navajo. The essence of this persistent structure is identified with elements of a basic Athabascan heritage of material and non-material elements reinterpreted through creative adaptations drawn from Pueblo cosmologies and ceremonial expressions.

Central to the Navajo view of the world and reality is the understanding that the human personality is a whole with every facet interrelated both within itself and in relationship to the totality of phenomena seen and unseen. Within this interrelated totality everything exists in two parts, the good and bad, the positive and negative, or the elements of male and female; they complement each other and belong together. Normally these elements are balanced, harmonious, ordered, and thus beautiful. This ideal equilibrium, however, is precarious and may be put out of balance through an indefinite number of possible

---

[2] E. H. Spicer, ed., *Navajo: Perspectives in American Culture Change* (Chicago: University of Chicago Press, 1961), pp. 278-336.

factors that must be avoided: doing anything to excess, the violation of taboos, contamination through contact with the ghosts of the dead, harboring evil thoughts, initiating or being the victim of acts of witchcraft, or any disrespect or carelessness in one's relationships with the forms and forces of a natural world that normally is in a state of balance and harmony.

Symptoms of any illness whatsoever are indications that the normal balance and harmony has been upset, and therefore must be restored. Such restoration of health for the Navajo person necessitates participation in one of several hundred ceremonial "chantways" of from two to nine or even fourteen days' duration. The chantway specific to the illness is determined by a special quasi-shaman diagnostician or "hand trembler." A singer (*hatali*) who knows the particular selected chantway is then contacted, and elaborate preparations are commenced. Sacred ceremonies must always be enacted within a *hogan*, the traditional Navajo circular or octagonal dwelling with an opening in the domed roof. Such dwellings, as well as the Athabascan-type conical sweat lodge, are considered by the people to be the world or cosmos, with its place of release in the opening above. Reminiscent of the Pueblos is the use of plumed prayer wands, which are set in the four directions outside the ceremonial *hogan* as a means to compel the *Yei* (gods) to come and be present with their curative spiritual powers. Central to the long and complex ceremonies within the *hogan* is the chanting by the singer of myths of creation, the episodes of heroes who purified the earth in primal times, or of other sacred mythic episodes that have specific relationship to the primary cause of the illness in question. These chants must be recited without any error of commission or omission whatsoever. At appropriate times, multicolored sand paintings are laid out with great precision on the clean sand of the *hogan* floor, upon the center of which the patient is seated so that the curative powers of the depicted gods, and of other beings and forms of power, may work for the restoration of harmony, balance, and thus health. Although the patient is the central beneficiary of these sacred rites, it is understood that powers thus generated spread out from the center to bless others who are present and eventually extend outward without limit.

Because the presiding ideal of their religious tradition is the maintenance of balance and harmony in interrelationships with the total environment, it is understandable that the Navajo are under considerable internal stress and tension in their confrontations with a surrounding world that is dominating, threatening, and unpredictable. Participation with this larger American world in foreign wars has intensified these pressures, even though the Navajo are very proud of their abilities in warfare, for slaying an enemy involves contact with the potentially dangerous ghost of the dead.

One avenue of controlled release from such tensions has long been the intensification on the reservation of witchcraft practices. Because such practices are institutionalized, they do not jeopardize the basic structures and foundations of Navajo life. Other types of possibly more positive responses are in a sense paradoxical, for they have resulted, on the one hand, in intensification of traditional ceremonial activities in order to "decontaminate" those who have been exposed to danger-ous forces associated with either the dead or the unfamiliar. On the other hand, and with the pragmatic sense that the Navajo have always shown, they now seek any available additional means for curing their ever-increasing and complex ailments. Here is found at least partial explanation for the Navajo's willing utilization of non-Indian health services, or for their increasing participation in the Native American Church, wherein their central focus is upon the use of the hallucino-genic peyote as curative agent.

Increased adherence to Christian denominations also involves iden-tification of the curative forces with Christian message. It is important to note, however, that historically the Catholic ministries have en-joyed less success among the Navajo than the Protestant or even Mor-mon missions, due to the fact that there is an incompatibility between core Navajo religious structures and the central rites of the Catholic Church. What is involved is not only the Navajo fear of contamina-tion with ghosts of the dead in relation to the crucifixion of Jesus, but also, the central rites of Holy Communion involve what to the Navajo are abhorrent acts of cannibalism. It remains to be seen in what man-ner the Navajo will be able to find ways through which the harmony and balance in their world can be maintained. Whatever resolutions or compromises are arrived at, it seems certain from past example that the people will continue to find ways through which their essential identity as Navajo is maintained.

CHRISTIAN "CONVERSION" AMONG AMERICAN INDIANS

The pervasive force of historical Christian ministries has probably had some impact upon all American Indian peoples. The gradations of Indian affiliation with Roman Catholicism and Protestant denomina-tions span two extremes: there are those who have fully accepted the new faith, accompanied by conscious rejection of their own religious traditions and even of their own languages, and those who have been exposed to elements of Christianity, or who even may once have totally accepted Christianity, but have since returned to an often intensified participation in their own sacred ways. Incomplete evidence suggests that these two groups constitute minorities in relation to those who are situated in unique manner between the two extremes. A key element in the evaluation of Indian affiliation with Christianity, to which sufficient attention has not been given in either scholarly literature or in church documents, lies in a special meaning of conversion for most American Indians, as indeed is the case for most representatives of the primal traditions who have had contact with Christianity.

The following perspective is fundamental to this inquiry. Throughout virtually all indigenous American Indian traditions, a pervasive theme has been that all forms and forces of all orders of the immediately experienced natural environment may communicate to human beings the totality of that which is to be known of the sacred mysteries of creation, and thus of the sacred essence of being and of beings. Orally transmitted sacred lore and accompanying ritual activities that have evolved from such cumulative personal and tribal experience assure the intensification and continuity of participation in the sacred. Such conditioning to openness of mind and being toward manifestations and experiences of the sacred makes it understandable that for these peoples religious matters of whatever origin are not open to either question or argument. When, therefore, the Christian message came to the peoples through dedicated missionaries who led exemplary and sacrificial lives, the people easily understood the truths of message and example due to the profundity of their own beliefs; it was not difficult for them to adopt and adapt new expressions of values into the sacred fabric of their own religious culture. The historical phenomenon is thus not conversion as understood in exclusivistic manner by the bearers of Christianity, but rather a continuation of the people's ancient and traditional facility for what may be termed non-exclusive cumulative adhesion. If this process of polysynthesis can be accomplished with neither confusion nor dissonance, it is ultimately due to the ability of American Indian peoples to penetrate and comprehend the central and most profound nature of all experience and reality. It may therefore be affirmed that American Indian living religions have the right to a legitimate place alongside the great religious traditions of the world.

CHAPTER 2

THE SPIRITUAL LEGACY

For centuries the American Indian peoples have been involved in a struggle that has taken on the proportions of a tragedy. It is a double tragedy, for it is ours as well as theirs, and it is still being enacted today. These original Americans have had, and fortunately still do have, great riches in human and spiritual resources. Yet these riches are either being swept aside and forgotten, or are being consciously and actively destroyed by a civilization that is out of balance precisely because it has lost those values. We give credit to the Indians for the discovery and development of foods, narcotics, and tobacco, yet we choose to forget what they never forgot, that we cannot live by bread alone. By ignoring or denying the spiritual legacy left to us by the Indians we have contributed to their impoverishment, and we have cut ourselves off from the possibility of an enrichment we desperately need.

Our consciences are relieved by a belief in such concepts as "progress," "manifest destiny," or the inevitability of our own way over all other life patterns, many of which have brought fulfillment, beauty, and dignity in a measure we cannot know so long as we continue in our present direction. In the history of humankind this conflict between cultures may be inevitable. And yet it is not inevitable that the American Indians give up the spiritual values and ritual practices of their ancient religions. Many Indians today, even among their young people and in spite of tremendous pressures brought against them from all sides, still find strength and meaning in their own religious beliefs and ceremonies. Those who remain faithful should be given every possible encouragement, because they are helping to keep alive a rich and truly American heritage that can be found nowhere else in the world, and that can provide values sorely needed by a culture seeking purpose and direction.

For the American Indians themselves, striving to adjust to new patterns of thinking and living, it is of crucial importance to rediscover and reaffirm their own heritage, for people cannot cut themselves off from what they really are without becoming as a tree without either roots or nourishment. Among the many forces at work to mold the Indian into a new image is our educational policy, which has been perpetuating a grave error in omitting from school curriculums almost everything that could and should affirm a heritage of great value; it could even be said that the policy was intentionally designed to destroy this unique heritage, and has thus risked creating people lacking either roots or purpose.

During the early contacts between Europeans and American aborigines the Indian was either depicted as a brutal savage, without civilization and possibly without a soul, or else was painted as an innocent child of nature, a type that is non-existent for the simple reason that humankind as a whole has lost the goodness of "paradise." The strictly ethnological accounts are of course more accurate and objective, but being a relative and specialized science, ethnology by its very nature is limited. An objective description of religious rites, social customs, or ritual paraphernalia may help us to catalogue and deduce certain conclusions but cannot give an insight into the spirituality many of the Indians knew and expressed in all facets of their culture.

As Frithjof Schuon, writing with great depth of understanding about the American Indian, has said recently:

> The fascinating combination of combative and stoical heroism and priestly bearing gave the Indian of the Plains and Forests something of the majesty of the eagle and the sun. This powerful and unique beauty of the Red Man contributes to his fame as a warrior and martyr. . . . If none of the so-called primitive peoples have given rise to as lively and lasting an interest as have the Red Indians, and if the Indian incarnates a certain nostalgia of ours which it would be wrong to call puerile, there must be some cause for it in the Indian himself, for "where there is smoke there is fire."[1]

There are times, to be sure, when our unfamiliarity with their symbolical forms, coupled with our own ethnocentricity, cause us to doubt whether American Indians had what we call "civilization," or whether they were developed enough to worship a Supreme Being approaching that which Christianity refers to as God. With our own overemphasis on mental activity we are apt to think that the Indian, without any written language, lacks something important or necessary in not possessing a scholastic or dialectical type of doctrinal presentation. However such a "lack" may have prevented *us* from understanding the completeness and depth of their wisdom, it represents for the

---

[1] "The Shamanism of the Red Indians," in *The Feathered Sun: Plains Indians in Art and Philosophy* (Bloomington, IN: World Wisdom Books, 1990), pp. 40-41, 41n.

Indians a very effective type of spiritual participation in which the essential ideas and values, reflected by a world of forms and symbols, are spontaneously and integrally *lived*. Undoubtedly Saint Bernard expressed something of the Indian's perspective when he said:

> What I know of the divine sciences and Holy Scripture, I learnt in woods and fields. I have had no other masters than the beeches and the oaks. Listen to a man of experience: thou wilt learn more in the woods than in books. Trees and stones will teach thee more than thou canst acquire from the mouth of a magister.

A further barrier to our understanding is our deep-rooted prejudice against the nomadic way of life many of the Indian groups followed. We are so blinded by the perspectives of our own society that we cannot realize that complex material achievements of the type we possess, or rather by which we are often possessed, are usually had at the expense of human and spiritual values. A minimum of material possessions does not necessarily mean a corresponding poverty in mental and spiritual achievements. The nomadic type of culture offers valuable lessons to the contemporary industrial person who is in danger of being crushed by the sheer weight of civilization, and who therefore often sacrifices the deepest and most meaningful values of life by identifying with an endless series of distracting and often destructive gadgets.

The material that is presented in this chapter is drawn from the traditions of the Indians of the Great Plains. The tribes of the Plains, with their unusual intellectuality, and with the great beauty and dignity of their cultural forms, represent an especially rich development among Amerindian peoples. It is not without reason that whenever the typical American Indian is to be represented it is usually the Plains Indian, with his magnificent fringed buckskin, eagle feathers, and quill decorations—all making for one of the most noble, dignified, and spectacular costumes to be found anywhere in the world. Another lifelong student of the American Indian, Hartley Burr Alexander, also emphasizes their unique position: "Under the great tutelage of Nature, noble and beautiful ceremonies were created, having at their hearts truths universal to mankind; and nowhere in America were such mysteries loftier and more impressive than among the tribes of the Great Plains."[2]

A second reason for concentrating on the Plains Indians is simply my familiarity with them. For over a year I had the opportunity of liv-

---

[2] *North American Mythology*, The Mythology of All Races series, vol. X (Boston, 1916, 1937), p. 77.

ing with an old man, Black Elk (*Hehaka Sapa*), who was a Lakota Sioux of the Pine Ridge Reservation in South Dakota. During this year Black Elk and his close friend Little Warrior freely told me about their religion and gave me the keys to the spiritual meaning behind the forms of their rites and symbols. This new understanding made clear to me why these old men, and others among their people, manifested in their being and in every act a nobility, serenity, generosity, concentration, and kindness that we usually associate with the saints of the better-known religions. Indeed it is in these two personalities that we have proof of the efficacy and reality of the Indian's spiritual methods and values.

I first learned of Black Elk through a remarkable book recorded by John Neihardt under the title *Black Elk Speaks* (1932). But it was not until 1948, after many months of travel, that I was able to find him living with his family in a little canvas tent in a migrant potato-picking camp in Nebraska. I well remember him as he sat on an old sheepskin hide, ill and pitiful, with his almost totally blind eyes staring beyond that which surrounded him. I sat beside him for some time, and still without speaking offered him a stone pipe filled with tobacco and *kinnikinnik* in the manner that I had been taught by old men of other tribes. We smoked in silence until finally, with a soft and kindly voice, he spoke in Lakota. His son translated. He surprised me by saying that he had anticipated my coming, was glad that I was there beside him, and asked if I would remain with him, for there was much that he would like to tell me before, as he said, he would "pass from this world of darkness into the other real world of light." I therefore returned with him to his log cabin on the reservation, lived with him and his generous family for almost a year, and from him and his friends I learned about the religion of his people. Every day he talked for several hours until a veil of silence fell in which one could sense that he was so absorbed within the realities of which he was speaking that words no longer had meaning. Indeed, the greater part of what I learned from Black Elk was not what he said, as valuable as this was, but what he was from his very being, which seemed to hover between this world of forms and the other world of the spirit. In all that he was there radiated an atmosphere that made one feel that one was in the presence of a holy man.

Although this sanctity and wholeness was evident in other old people among the Sioux, there was in Black Elk some special quality that set him apart from his people. From the early age of nine he had received visions with an unusual frequency and intensity, so that under their power he lived with the burning compulsion to help his people by bringing back to life the "flowering tree" of their religious heritage. This tree had once flourished and borne fruit at the center of their nation, but now it had withered and Black Elk knew not what to do.

> With tears running, O Great Spirit, Great Spirit, my Grandfather—with running tears I must say now that the tree has never bloomed. A pitiful old man, you see here, and I have fallen away and have done nothing. Here at the center of the world, where you took me when I was young and taught me; here, old, I stand, and the tree is withered, Grandfather, my Grandfather!
>
> Again, and maybe the last time on this earth, I recall the great vision you sent me. It may be that some little root of the sacred tree still lives. Nourish it then, that it may leaf and bloom and fill with singing birds. Hear me, not for myself, but for my people; I am old. Hear me that they may once more go back into the sacred hoop and find the good red road, the shielding tree.[3]

Because of this mission to keep alive his religious heritage, Black Elk wished to pass on to his people and to the world those aspects of his religion that were recorded in *Black Elk Speaks*, and in the book I recorded for him in 1953, *The Sacred Pipe*. It is in keeping with his wish, and for the sake of the values themselves, that I present the following material.

One of the symbols that expresses most completely the Plains Indian concept of the relationship between human beings and the world of nature surrounding them is a cross inscribed within a circle. The symbol is painted on a number of ritual objects, and on the bodies and heads of people who participate in tribal ceremonies. Its form is reflected in the circular shape and central fire of the tipi, the Indian's home; its pattern is found in the Sun Dance and purification lodges and in many of the ritual movements. For example, in the Hako ceremony of the Pawnee, the priest draws a circle on the earth with his toe: "The circle represents a nest, and is drawn by the toe, because the Eagle [symbol of the Great Mysterious] builds its nest with its claws. Although we are imitating the bird making its nest, there is another meaning to the action; we are thinking of *Tirawa* making the world for the people to live in."[4]

---

[3] Black Elk, as told to John G. Neihardt, *Black Elk Speaks* (New York, 1932), pp. 279-280. Reprinted in paperback by the Bison Series of the University of Nebraska, 1961.

[4] Alice C. Fletcher, *The Hako: A Pawnee Ceremony*, annual report of the Bureau of American Ethnology, XXII, ii, 1904.

In complaining that the Indian must now live in a *square* log house, a form without power to the Indians, Black Elk once said:

> You have noticed that everything an Indian does is in a circle, and that is because the Power of the World always works in circles, and everything tries to be round. In the old days when we were a strong and happy people, all our power came to us from the sacred hoop of the nation, and so long as the hoop was unbroken, the people flourished. The flowering tree was the living center of the hoop, and the circle of the four quarters nourished it. The east gave peace and light, the south gave warmth, the west gave rain, and the north with its cold and mighty wind gave strength and endurance. This knowledge came to us from the outer world with our religion. Everything the Power of the World does is done in a circle. The sky is round, and I have heard that the earth is round like a ball, and so are all the stars. The wind, in its greatest power, whirls. Birds make their nests in circles, for theirs is the same religion as ours. The sun comes forth and goes down again in a circle. The moon does the same, and both are round. Even the seasons form a great circle in their changing, and always come back again to where they were. The life of a man is a circle from childhood to childhood, and so it is in everything where power moves. Our teepees were round like the nests of birds, and these were always set in a circle, the nation's hoop, a nest of many nests, where the Great Spirit meant for us to hatch our children.[5]

At the center of the circle, uniting within a point the four directions of the cross and all the other quaternaries of the Universe, is a human person. Without the awareness that they bear within themselves this sacred center, human beings are in fact less than human. It is to recall the virtual reality of this center that the Indians have so many rites based on the cross within the circle.

One of the most precise ritual expressions of this "centrality" is found in one of the rites of the Arapaho Sun Dance, in which their Sacred Wheel is placed against each of the four sides of a man's body, starting from the feet and moving to the head, and is then turned sunwise four times, until finally it is lowered over the head, with the four attached eagle feathers hanging down over the man's breast, so that he is ritually at the center, a vertical axis to the horizontal wheel.

This concept of the vertical axis explains the sacredness of the number seven to the Indians, and it is interesting to note that their interpretation is identical to that found in other major religions. In add-

---

[5] *Black Elk Speaks*, pp. 198-200.

ing the vertical dimensions of sky and earth to the four horizontal ones of space, we have six dimensions, with the seventh as the point at the center where all the directions meet.

To realize this symbol in its fullness we must conceive of three horizontal circles inscribed with crosses, all three pierced by the vertical axis of humanity itself. For the Indians understand that human beings are intermediate between sky and earth, linking the two, with feet on the ground and the head, or intellect, at the center of the firmament. The middle disc, like the vertical axis, represents humanity, for in joining sky and earth, it is neither pure spirit nor gross matter, but a synthesis of both. This particular symbol may be found among the Crow in the three rings they often paint around the sacred cottonwood tree at the center of their circular Sun Dance lodge. It was further explained to me by an old Crow priest or medicine man that these circles represent the three "worlds" that constitute human beings: body, soul, and spirit, or again: gross, subtle, and pure.

Once this concept of humanity and its relationship to the universe has been understood, one is able to understand the Indians approach to the forms of virgin nature that surrounded them, and which they knew so intimately. In most of the great religious traditions of the world people built centers of worship in the form of cathedrals, churches, or temples, and in these centers and in the many symbolical forms introduced into them, people expressed their image of the universe. It is certainly not difficult to sense this totality, or to feel that one is actually at the center of the world when one is inside the great medieval cathedrals of Europe. For the Indians, however, the world of nature itself was their temple, and within this sanctuary they showed great respect to every form, function, and power. That the Indians held as sacred all the natural forms surrounding them is not unique, for other traditions (Japanese Shinto, for example) respect created forms as manifestations of God's works. But what is almost unique in the Indians' attitude is that their reverence for nature and for life is *central* to their religion: each form in the world around them bears such a host of precise values and meanings that taken all together they constitute what one would call their "doctrine."

In my first contacts with Black Elk almost all that he said was phrased in terms involving animals and natural phenomena. I naively wished that he would begin to talk about religious matters, until I finally realized that he was, in fact, explaining his religion. The values I sought were to be found precisely in his stories and accounts of the bison, eagle, trees, flowers, mountains, and winds.

Due to this intense preoccupation with the forms of nature, Indians have been described as being in their religion either pantheistic, idolatrous, or downright savage. It is hardly necessary to reply to the two latter terms, but the more subtle charge of pantheism, which involves equating God with manifested forms, requires some clarification.

In the extremely beautiful creation myths of the Plains Indians, which are amazingly similar to the biblical Genesis, the animals were created before human beings, so that in their anteriority and divine origin they have a certain proximity to the Great Spirit (*Wakan-Tanka* in the language of the Sioux), which demands respect and veneration. In them the Indian sees actual reflections of the qualities of the Great Spirit, which serve the same function as revealed scriptures in other religions. They are intermediaries or links between human beings and God. This explains not only why religious devotions may be directed to the deity *through* the animals, but it also helps us to understand why contact with, or from, the Great Spirit, comes to the Indian almost exclusively through visions involving animal or other natural forms. Black Elk, for example, received spiritual power (*wochangi*) from visions involving the eagle, the bison, Thunder-beings, and horses; and it is said that Crazy Horse, the great chief and holy man, received his power and invulnerability from the rock, and also from a vision of the shadow.

Although these natural forms may reflect aspects of the Great Spirit, and eventually cannot be other than the Great Spirit, they are nevertheless not identified with He "who is without Parts," and who in His transcendent unity is above all particular created forms. The Indian therefore cannot be termed a pantheist, if we accept this term in the usual sense. Black Elk has formulated well this mystery in the following statement:

> . . . We regard all created beings as sacred and important, for everything has a *wochangi*, or influence, which can be given to us, through which we may gain a little more understanding if we are attentive. We should understand well that all things are the works of the Great Spirit. We should know that He is within all things; the trees, the grasses, the rivers, the mountains and all the four-legged animals, and the winged peoples; and even more important, we should understand that He is also above all these things and peoples.[6]

---

[6] Joseph Epes Brown, *The Sacred Pipe* (Norman, Oklahoma: University of Oklahoma, 1953), pp. xx, 59.

To make these distinctions more precise, it should be noted that in the language of the Sioux (Lakota), the Great Spirit may be referred to as either Father (*Ate*) or Grandfather (*Tunkashila*). *Ate* refers to the Great Spirit in relation to His creation, in other words, as Being, whereas *Tunkashila* is the non-manifest essence, independent of the limitations of creation. These same distinctions have been enunciated by Christian theologians using the term God as distinct from Godhead, and in the Hindu doctrines that differentiate between Brahma (the masculine form) and Brahman (the neuter form).

In recalling the symbol of the circle, cross, and central axis, we can now see that although humans were created last of all the creatures, they are also the "axis," and thus in a sense the first. For if each animal reflects particular aspects of the Great Spirit, human beings, on the contrary, may include within themselves all the aspects. A human being is thus a totality, bearing the Universe within himself or herself and through the intellect having the potential capacity to live in continual awareness of this reality. As Black Elk has said: "Peace . . . comes within the souls of men when they realize their relationship, their oneness, with the universe and all its powers, and when they realize that at the center of the Universe dwells *Wakan-Tanka*, and that this center is really everywhere, it is within each of us."[7]

The Indian believes that such knowledge cannot be realized unless there is perfect humility, unless human beings humble themselves before the entire creation, before the smallest ant, realizing their own nothingness. Only in being nothing may an individual human being become everything, and only then realize the essential kinship with all forms of life. A human being's center, or Life, is the same center or Life of all that is.

Because of humankind's totality and centrality it has the almost divine function of guardianship over the world of nature. Once this role is ignored or misused people are in danger of being shown ultimately by nature who in reality is the conqueror and who the conquered. It could also be said, from another perspective, that in the past humans had to protect themselves from the forces of nature, whereas today it is nature that must be protected from humans.

Nothing is more tragic or pitiful than the statements of Indians who have survived to see their sacred lands torn up and desecrated by a people of an alien culture who, driven largely by commercial inter-

---

[7] *The Sacred Pipe*, p. 115.

ests, have lost the sense of protective guardianship over nature. Typical are the words of an old Omaha:

> When I was a youth, the country was very beautiful. Along the rivers were belts of timberland, where grew cottonwood, maple, elm, ash, hickory, and walnut trees, and many other shrubs. And under these grew many good herbs and beautiful flowering plants. In both the woodland and the prairies I could see the trails of many kinds of animals and could hear the cheerful songs of many kinds of birds. When I walked abroad I could see many forms of life, beautiful living creatures which *Wakanda* had placed here; and these were, after their manner, walking, flying, leaping, running, playing all about. But now the face of all the land is changed and sad. The living creatures are gone. I see the land desolate and I suffer an unspeakable sadness. Sometimes I wake in the night and I feel as though I should suffocate from the pressure of this awful feeling of loneliness.[8]

Too often statements such as this are passed off as nostalgic romanticism, but if we understand the full meaning of the world of nature for the Indian, we realize that we are involved witnesses to a great tragedy, whose final act is still to be seen.

The remarkable spiritual development to be found among many of the Plains Indians derives not only from their close contact with nature, but also through rigorous participation in a multitude of rites and symbols of a supernatural origin, which are often of great complexity. Through participation in these rites, which have been faithfully transmitted from generation to generation, the Indian comes to know, to understand, and then to seek those values reflected in the great mirror of nature. Far from being simple and passive "children of nature," the Indians have dynamic personalities of great force, courage, and intelligence, and often undergo intense suffering and sacrifice in becoming what they are and in preserving what they have.

Through people such as Black Elk, Little Warrior, Standing Bear, *Ohiyesa* (Charles Eastman), and others, we are able to understand the wisdom in their rites and cultural forms. We know of the sacred power they individually received when they made their religious retreats (*hanblecheyapi*), alone on high mountain tops, going for four days or more without food or water, and praying continually that the Great

---

[8] Melvin R. Gilmore, *Prairie Smoke* (New York: Columbia University Press, 1929), p. 36.

Spirit might hear and in compassion send one of His messengers in a vision.

In the religious retreat the Indian as an individual sought spiritual renewal, whereas in the rites of the annual spring Sun Dance (*Wiwanyag Wachipi*) the entire tribe gathered to ensure renewal not only of the participating individual, but of the tribe itself, of the world, and of the Universe. This four-day ritual dance is also still practiced by most of the Plains Indians, even though many of the forms have been modified and simplified under pressures from missionaries and the "civilizing" influences of our modern world. The essential power and functions of the Sun Dance, however, are still present, and anybody who has observed the complete three- or four-day ceremony cannot but be impressed, and deeply moved, by the otherworldly beauty of the sacred songs, by the powerful rhythm of the great drum struck simultaneously by many men, by the directness in the geometry of the ritual movements of the dancers (which again is based on the relationship between the circle and its axis or center), and by the aspects of duration and sacrifice.

To illustrate in some detail at least one of the Plains Indians ceremonies I have chosen the purification rites of the sweat lodge, the *Inipi*. These rites are carried out in preparation for all the other major rites, and actually are participated in prior to any important undertaking. They are rites of renewal, or spiritual rebirth, in which each of the four elements—earth, air, fire, and water—contribute to the people's physical and psychical purification.

A small dome-shaped lodge is first made of bent willow saplings over which are placed buffalo hides, which make the little house tight and dark inside. Within the lodge, and at its center, there is a small pit containing rocks that have already been heated in a fire outside the lodge to the east. When the leader of the ceremony sprinkles water on these they give off steam, so that soon the lodge becomes intensely hot, and also fragrant from the aromatic sage strewn on the floor. Each of the materials in the lodge has its symbolic value, as does every detail of design and ritual usage.

Black Elk, among others, has explained that the lodge itself represents the Universe, with the pit at the center as the navel in which dwells the Great Spirit with His power, which is the fire. The willows that form the frame of the house represent all that grows from Mother Earth.

> These too have a lesson to teach us, for in the fall their leaves die and return to the earth, but in the spring they come to life again. So,

too, men die but live again in the real world of *Wakan-Tanka*, where there is nothing but the spirits of all things; and this true life we may know here on earth if we purify our bodies and minds, thus coming closer to *Wakan-Tanka* who is all-purity.[9]

The rocks represent the earth, and also the indestructible and everlasting nature of *Wakan-Tanka*. The water, too, reflects values for the people to learn from:

When we use water in the sweat lodge we should think of *Wakan-Tanka* who is always flowing, giving His power and life to everything; we should even be as water which is lower than all things, yet stronger even than the rocks.[10]

It is important to note that to the Plains Indian the material form of the symbol is not thought of as representing some *other* and higher reality, but *is* that reality in an image. The power or quality, therefore, that a particular form reflects may be transferred directly to the person in contact with it, and there is no need, as with modern Western people, for any mental or artificial "reconstruction." It may even be said that the Indian can be passive to the form, and is thus able to absorb, and become one with, its reflected power.

During the four periods of sweating within the lodge, prayers are recited, sacred songs are sung, and a pipe is ceremonially smoked four times by the circle of people. At the conclusion of the fourth and last period the door is opened so that "the light enters into the darkness, that we may see not only with our two eyes, but with the one eye which is of the heart, and with which we see and know all that is true and good." Going forth into the light from the house of darkness, in which all impurities have been left behind, represents human liberation from ignorance, from the ego, and from the cosmos. The person is now a renewed being entering symbolically into the world of light or wisdom.

There is in these rites an amazing completeness. In other great religions one, or sometimes two, of the elements are used for purification or consecration. Here four of the elements are present (one could include the fifth "element": ether) in such a powerfully interrelated

9 *The Sacred Pipe*, pp. 31-32.

10 *The Sacred Pipe*, p. 31.

manner that one cannot but believe that for each participating individual the goal, in varying degrees, must be achieved.

As a thread binds together, and is central to, each bead of a necklace, so is the sacred pipe central to all the Plains Indian ceremonies. The pipe is a portable altar, and a means of grace, that every Indian once possessed. He would not undertake anything of importance unless he had first smoked, concentrating on all that the pipe represented, and thus absorbing a multitude of powers. It could in fact be said that if one could understand all the possible meanings and values to be found in the pipe and its accompanying ritual, then one could understand Plains Indian religion in its full depth.

The origin of the pipe is expressed in various myths of great beauty. In the Sioux myth a miraculous Buffalo Cow Woman brought the pipe to the people, with explanations concerning its meaning and use. Pipes used in historical times, and still used today, are made with a red, or sometimes a black, stone bowl, a stem usually of ash, and—at least with the large ceremonial types—ribbon decorations representing the four directions of space, and parts taken from sacred animals or from nature. These pipes represent the human being in his totality, or the universe of which humankind is a reflection. The bowl is the heart, or sacred center, and each section of the pipe is usually identified with some part of the human being.

As the pipe is filled with the sacred tobacco, prayers are offered for all the powers of the universe, and for the myriad forms of creation, each of which is represented by a grain of tobacco. The filled pipe is thus Totality, so that when the fire of the Great Spirit is added, a divine sacrifice is enacted in which the Universe and humankind are reabsorbed within the Principle, and become what in reality they are. In mingling life-breath with the tobacco and fire through the straight stem of concentration, the person who smokes assists at the sacrifice of the self or ego, and is thus aided in realizing the Divine Presence at his or her own center. Indeed, in the liberation of the smoke one is helped not only to find God's presence within, but to realize that oneself and the world are mysteriously plunged in God. The smoke that rises to the heavens is also, as it were, visible prayer, at the sight and fragrance of which the entire creation rejoices. The mysteries of the peace pipe are so profound that the rite of smoking for the Indian can be compared to the Holy Communion for Christians. It is therefore not without reason that it is commonly called a "peace pipe," and was always used in establishing a relationship, or peace, between friends and also enemies. For in smoking the pipe together each person is aided in remembering his or her own center, which is now understood to be the same center of every other person, and of the Universe itself. It would be difficult to imagine a rite that could more aptly express the bond that exists among all forms of creation.

All true spiritual progress involves three stages, which are not successfully experienced and left behind, but rather each in turn is realized and then integrated within the next stage, so that ultimately they become one in the individual who attains the ultimate goal. Different terms may be used for these stages, but essentially they constitute purification, perfection or expansion, and union.

If union with Truth (which is one of many possible names for God) is the ultimate goal of all spiritual disciplines, then it is evident that what is impure cannot be united with that which is all-purity. Hence the necessity for the first stage of purification. Expansion follows because only that which is perfect, total, or whole can be united with absolute perfection and holiness. One must cease to be a part, an imperfect fragment; one must also realize what one really is so as to expand to include the Universe within oneself. Only then, when these two conditions of purification and expansion are actualized, may one attain to the final stage of union. All the great religions attest that there is no greater error to which human beings are subject than to regard the real self as nothing more than the body or the mind. It is only through traditional disciplines, such as those that have been described for the Plains Indian, that people are able to dispel this greatest of all illusions.

The pattern of the three stages in spiritual development may be recognized in one form or another in the methods of all the great religions of the world. It is evident that the American Indian, or at least the Plains Indian, also possesses this same threefold pattern of realization. If this spirituality has not as yet been fully recognized as existing among the Indians, it is due partly to a problem of communication, since their conceptions are often expressed through symbolic forms that are foreign to us. If we can understand, however, the truths the Indians find in their relationships to nature, and the profound values reflected by their many rites and symbols, then *we* may become enriched, our understanding will deepen, and we shall be able to give to the American Indian heritage its rightful place among the great spiritual traditions of humankind. Further, if Indians themselves can become more actively aware of this valuable heritage, then they may regain much of what has been lost, and will be able to face the world with the pride and dignity that should rightfully be theirs.

CHAPTER 3

THE ROOTS OF RENEWAL

There is an unprecedented explosion of interest today in all facets of the Native American heritage. It is especially significant that this interest and concern are shared by the Native American and the non-Native American alike. Analyses of the complex reasons for this concern is outside the scope of this book. But it may be suggested that what underlies it all is the Native American's increasing disenchantment with the world that for centuries has been presented as the ultimate model of true civilization. Paralleling this disenchantment of Native Americans is the non-Native American's questioning of many of the basic premises of their own civilization. Both Indian and non-Indian are engaged in a quest for the roots of lost heritages now increasingly understood to be essential if we are to reorient our cultures and lives toward values that express real human nature. In this mutual quest many Native American groups are far closer to their sources than are non-Natives. And so perhaps for the first time in history we are allowing, even asking them to talk, so that we may listen and learn. Hope lies in the possibility of a true dialogue wherein each may learn from the other, so that each may come to know himself or herself. We are essentially all engaged in the same kind of process, each in our own way asking the same kinds of fundamental questions.

The causes for the new search for the roots of lost traditions, and for self-examination and reevaluation, are at once both simple and vastly complex. They are obvious yet elusive. But if the root causes of the situation are grasped, or at least partially identified, it may be possible better to understand a multitude of present events, movements, and phenomena that are unfolding with increasing intensity. New manifestations of Indian militancy may be responsible for increased public awareness. But such action-oriented movements certainly neither define nor resolve the root causes of the problems. It would thus be superficial to assert, as has often been suggested, that action-oriented techniques are primarily responsible for the current renewal or reformulation of elements of a people's traditional heritage.

Many Native American groups have learned over generations of bitter experiences to preserve their sacred traditions underground. Some of the current "renewal," therefore, simply represents the current willingness of the people to give greater visibility to their sacred rites and beliefs, which have been kept hidden from a materially dominant world intent on destroying these very traditions.

It seems to me that we are faced today with a pervasive process, on a global scale, of detraditionalization or despiritualization. The world has been experiencing this process in a cumulative manner for many centuries. Exceedingly complex historical causes are no doubt responsible. As this process of detraditionalization has proceeded, its influence has demanded that the basic premises and orientations of our society be reevaluated. Detraditionalization has had an impact on the integrity of virtually all Native American traditions or life-ways. The reevaluation by Native American peoples of their own conditions involves an assessment of their relationships to the materially dominant society. Frequently, when sincere attempts are made by Native Americans to adjust to or acculturate within the dominant society, they become involved in a process of diminishing returns, or reach dead ends with regard to acquiring a meaningful quality of life.

The struggle of both Indians and non-Indians to find answers to their respective situations has led increasingly to attempts to regain contact with the roots of their traditions. Since their indigenous traditions are deeply and intricately rooted in this very land, unlike the more recently transplanted Europeans, the Indians have a certain advantage in this quest. It is understandable that non-Native people—especially among the younger generations—who once looked everywhere except to their own homeland for answers are now increasingly turning to Native Americans and their traditions for possible alternatives to the values of their own society. To them these values have come to represent an impoverished reality. The great hope in this dual search of Indians and non-Indians is that a true and open dialogue may be established through which neither will attempt to imitate the other, but where each may ultimately regain and reaffirm the sacred dimensions of *their own* respective traditions.

In spite of the vast differences among the sacred traditions of the native cultures of North America, it is nevertheless possible to identify certain core or root themes that seem to undergird the traditions of all these groups, even though they are expressed through a rich diversity of means.

TIME

Within traditional Native American cultures, time tends to be experienced as cyclical and rhythmic rather than as linear and "progress"-

oriented. The rhythm of the world in its mode of operation is believed to be circular, as is the life of a human or of any manifested form or being. Events or processes transmitted through oral traditions tend not to be recounted in terms of time past or time future in the linear sense. Indeed most Native American languages do not have past and future tenses; they reflect rather a perennial reality of the now. The rich mythic accounts of creation, for example, do not tell of chronological time past, but of processes that are eternally happening. The same processes are recurring now and are to recur in other future cycles.

Given this structure of experience that is supported by the forms of language and made immediate through experienced interrelationships with the elements of each people's natural environment, it is impossible in Native American thought to conceive of progress in the non-Indian linear sense—that quantitatively interpreted cumulative process in which the more and the new are mysteriously and automatically identified with the better. However, the forces and events asserting themselves upon us at this moment in our history increasingly demand a backward look at progress so that its premises may be reexamined critically. Through such reexamination and, possibly, reorientation, Native American traditions may serve as a reminder of forgotten or neglected dimensions latent within European America's own heritage. For example, we know that at one time this heritage also manifested a dependence on sacred time.

PLACE

If alternatives are being sought today to our pervasive linear, progress-laden concepts of time, there is also the parallel quest for a new understanding and appreciation of place. Native American affirmations of the interrelated sacredness of time and place are spelled out across our land with enormous creative diversity. Yet all of it exhibits some fundamental common principles.

Native American experiences of place are infused with mythic themes. These express events of sacred time, which are as real now as at any other time. They are experienced through landmarks in each people's immediate natural environment. The events of animal beings, for example, which are communicated through oral traditions of myths or folklore, serve to grace, sanctify, explain, and interpret each detail of the land. Further, each being of nature, every particular form of the land, is experienced as the locus of qualitatively differentiated spirit beings, whose individual and collective presence sanctifies and gives meaning to the land in all its details and contours. Thus, it also gives meaning to the lives of people who cannot conceive of themselves apart from the land. Such beliefs in a plurality of indwelling spirits (often referred to rather unkindly as "animism" or "animatism") must be understood in relation to a polysynthetic quality of vision. The recognition of multiplicity on one level of reality need not militate against the coalescing of the omnipresent spirit beings within a more ultimate unitary principle. Such a polysynthetic metaphysic of nature, immediately experienced rather than dangerously abstracted, speaks with particular force to the root causes of many of today's problems, especially to our present so-called ecological crisis. It is perhaps this message of the sacred nature of the land, of place, that today has been most responsible for forcing the Native American vision upon the mind and conscience of the non-Native American.

Such affirmation and experience of sacred time and sacred place wherever these may be found tend to free humanity from the oppressive limits of profane time and profane place. Experiencing such constriction and thus inevitably feeling nostalgia for what has been lost, people today have come to seek the illusion of liberation through explorations of outer space. This quest is futile, of course, especially if embarked upon to satisfy ultimate concerns, since even such seemingly limitless reaches of space, being always of a material and thus quantitative order, are still within the domain of limitation. Such attempts by contemporary humans to "conquer" time and space, even to "conquer" specific places, are incomprehensible to Native Americans, particularly to Native American or arctic shamans. These shamans, through the non-material means of their sacred traditions, are able to travel at will through the freedom of sacred space unfettered by mechanical, profane time.

Not only Native Americans but traditional-oriented peoples, wherever they may be, always found the means by which to be protected from the indefiniteness of space. The tipi, the *hogan*, or the longhouse—like the temple, the cathedral, or the sacred city center of antiquity—determined the perimeters of space in such a way that a sacred place, or enclosure, was established. Space so defined served as a model of the world, of the universe, or, microcosmically, of a human being. Essential to such definition of space, so central to human need, were means by which the centers of sacred space or place were established. For without such ritual fixing of a center there can be no circumference. And with neither circumference nor center where does a person stand? A ritually defined center, whether the fire at the center of the Plains tipi or the *sipapu* (earth navel) within the Pueblo *kiva*, obviously expresses not just a mathematically fixed point established arbitrarily in space. It is also taken to be the actual center of the world. It is understood as an axis serving as a bridge between heaven and earth, an axis that pierces through a multiplicity of worlds. The great cottonwood tree at the center of (and branching out above) the Plains Sun Dance lodge is this central axis. It symbolizes the way of liberation from the limits of the cosmos. Vertical ascent is impossible unless the starting point is the ritual center. Here again such primordial types of formulations found within our American land may serve as reminders to those who have lost or forgotten the sense of a center.

RELATIONSHIP

One key to the Native American religious perspective, which again speaks to a quality of life sought by contemporary generations in their loss of center and concomitant sense of alienation and fragmentation, may be found in Native American concepts of relationship, all orders of which are richly defined and supported by the forms of language and by specific ritual means. Relationships between members of family, band, clan, or tribal groups tend to be defined, and thus intensified, through relational or generational terms rather than through personal names which are considered to be sacred and thus private to the individual. This sense of relationship pertains not only to members of a nuclear family, band, or clan. It also extends outward to include all beings of the specific environment, the elements, and the winds, whether these beings, forms, or powers are what we would call animate or inanimate. In Native American thought no such hard dichotomies exist. All such forms under creation are understood to be mysteriously interrelated. Everything is relative to every other being or thing; thus, nothing exists in isolation. The intricately interrelated threads of the spider's web are used as a metaphor for the world. The same reference occurs in Native American art. This is a profound symbol, when it is understood. The people observed that the threads of the web were drawn out from within the spider's very being. They also recognized that the threads in concentric circles were sticky, whereas the threads leading to the center were smooth!

One vivid example of this comprehensive sense of relationship is expressed with special force among the Plains peoples in rites involving communal smoking of the pipe. At the conclusion of the pipe ceremony among the Lakota the participants all exclaim: "We are all related!" What is acknowledged here is not only the relatedness of the immediate participating group. There is also an affirmation of the mysterious interrelatedness of all that is. The rites of the pipe specifically mention that each of the indefinite number of grains of tobacco placed in the bowl of the pipe represents ritually, or really *is*, some specific form or possibility of creation. The act of smoking then is a rite of communion. Through the agency of human breath the apparent multiplicity and separateness of phenomena (the tobacco) is absorbed within an ultimate unity (the fire).

If new life is being given to such rites as communal pipe-smoking among Native American peoples today, or to any similar means for the reaffirmation of relationship, belonging, and identity, it is entirely understandable. Many Native Americans are drawn to such expressions because they have either been denied truly meaningful relationships with the dominant society, or have found frustration in a society where experience is so excessively and artificially fragmented.

THE ORAL TRADITIONS

Perhaps the greatest tragedy to come upon Native American groups has been the progressive weakening and occasional total loss of their respective languages. Since language supports and communicates the total range of a people's values and world view, it was realized early by the dominant society that Native American languages must be supplanted by the language of the dominant society if cultural assimilation was to occur. The history of the frequent brutal means by which this process of deculturation was furthered need not be reiterated here. We must stress the fact, however, that due to the inherent persistence of language many Native American languages have survived. Furthermore, many Native American groups are taking deliberate measures to insure that these languages are both recovered and used.

These procedures are being assisted by the increasing control Native Americans are exercising with respect to their own educational systems. Where such languages are alive, oral traditions can be revitalized to communicate the core values to all members of the group. Some segments of the dominant society, which has always placed a very high premium on literacy and on the linear perspective—in this case the written line—have finally begun to recognize the powerful effectiveness of oral transmission for educational purposes. The importance given to the "frame"—that is, the time, the season, and the immediate environment within which the narration takes place—serves to place, reinforce, and intensify what is communicated. Regardless of the type of myth or folktale, multiple levels of understanding are always possible. This enables the narration to speak specifically and simultaneously to all age groups present. Normally in tribal societies the elders of experience serve as repositories for the oral lore of the people. Living oral traditions give the elders of the society a position of respect and importance. Further, since oral tradition speaks even to the youngest in the group, it creates bridges of understanding between the generations. Oral tradition can thus be addressed with special force to problems of generational segmentation and individual alienation so typical of much of the American world today.

It is a trait of the southwestern Pueblo peoples to objectify the realities and dynamics of experience through the *kachinas*, sometimes called "gods." There is an account of a Zuni *kachina* who emerged from the underworld attached back to back with a person from an alien world. Back to back, it was suggested, the alien is destined neither to see nor to understand the Zuni. Yet the fact remains that the two are attached. If there is hope, it lies in the possibility that there may come a time for a turning around, so that each may know who the other is and what the other might become.

CHAPTER 4

THE PERSISTENCE OF ESSENTIAL VALUES

To examine the complex question of the persistence of essential traditional values among American Indian groups, we shall focus on the
Indians of the Great Plains of North America. This selection in a sense
is arbitrary, for similar studies could well be extended to almost any of
the American Indian groups scattered in reservations throughout the
United States, many of whom still retain, underneath the more evident
surface changes and adaptations, world views and life-ways still deeply
rooted in ancient values. Since my closest personal contacts, however,
have been with the Plains tribes such as the Sioux, Cheyenne, Crow,
Blackfoot, Arapaho, and Shoshone, I have chosen to look to these cultures for evidence of persistence of essential traditional values.

The use of the term "essential values" in this context refers to
transcendent metaphysical principles central to the spiritual ways of
the Plains Indians, which constitute for these original Americans an
expression of what has been called the *religio perennis.* The uniqueness,
or possibly strangeness, to us of the Indian's ritual forms or symbolical
language should never blind us to the universal quality of the underlying values themselves. The survival of the values themselves is not in
question, for being ultimately timeless and eternal they can never in
themselves be qualified by the vicissitudes of the socio-cultural environment. The question, rather, is the degree to which changes imposed
by an alien and generally profane culture will allow these values to
continue to operate within a changing cultural matrix and thus within
the human substance of the individual.

This chapter will first describe selected indigenous core values of
the Plains Indians as they are conveyed through their ritual supports,
and thus as they contribute to methods of spiritual realization. This
necessarily synthetic treatment provides a reference base for the second part of the chapter, which will deal with several dimensions in the
dynamics of contact, as the indigenous culture confronts the pervasive
and disruptive influences issuing from a materially dominant Anglo-
American culture.

VALUES

Among the many sacred ceremonies of the Plains Indians, three major
rituals—separately and in their totality—exemplify all necessary

dimensions of a true way of spiritual realization for the individual and for the social group as a whole. These rites are those of purification, the annual tribal Sun Dance, and the individual spiritual retreat.

The rites of purification, considered to be essential preparation for any important or sacred undertaking, have been described to some extent on pp. 31-32. To elaborate further, the domed shaped sweat lodge is said to symbolize the very body of the Great Spirit. Inside this lodge participants submit themselves to intensely hot steam. As the people pray and chant, the steam, actually conceived as the visible image of the Great Spirit, acts as in an alchemical work to dissolve both physical and psychic "coagulations" so that a spiritual transmutation may take place. The four elements with the invisible spiritual Presence—or "fifth element"—contribute their respective powers to this purifying process so that the individual may become truly whole by first dissolving the illusory sense of separateness, then becoming reintegrated, or harmoniously unified, within the totality of the universe. In finally going forth from the dark lodge, leaving behind all physical impurities and spiritual errors, a person is reborn into the wisdom of the light of day. All aspects of the world have been witnesses to this cycle of corruption, death, wholeness, and rebirth; indeed, the cosmic powers have all contributed to the process.

In the rites of the Sun Dance (see pp. 12-13 and 77-80) there is a shift in perspective and function. These dramatic and powerful rites, normally of four days' duration, are generally performed only once annually, and are participated in, directly or indirectly, by the entire tribal group. A major overt goal of this prayer dance is the regeneration or renewal not only of the individual directly participating in the rites, but also of the tribe and ultimately of the entire universe.

Blowing on whistles made from the wing bone of the eagle, the men dance individually with simple and dignified steps toward the central tree from which they receive supernatural power, and then dance backward to the periphery of the circle without shifting their gaze from the center. The sacred forms and ritual actions are virile, dignified, and direct. The power of the sacred center, now realized within the people themselves, remains throughout the year with each individual and contributes to their unity.

The third spiritual way is the solitary retreat known as the "lamenting," or the vision quest. In this quest the individual, naked and alone, and in constant prayer, endures a total fast for a specified number of days at a lonely place, usually a mountain top. In utter humility of body and mind, often emphasized by the offering of pieces of his flesh or the joint of a finger, the individual stands before the forms and forces of nature seeking the blessing of sacred power which should come to him through a dream, or preferably a vision, of some aspect of nature, possibly an animal, who offers guidance for the future direction of the individual's life. These natural forms or forces, conceived as messengers or agents, constitute for the Indian a well-understood "iconography" in which forms, with their accompanying powers, are ranked according to their ability to express most directly the ultimate Power, or essence, of the Great Spirit. Essential to this metaphysic of nature is the Indian's belief that in silence, found within the solitude of nature, there is ultimately heard the very voice of the Great Spirit. This quest for supernatural power, symbolically coming from the "outside" but in reality being awakened from within, has always been essential to the spiritual life of Plains Indian men and women, and its influence on the quality of their lives should never be underestimated.

Finally, mention must be made of the sacred tobacco pipe which is an important ritual implement central to all three rites. In this portable altar the Indian has access at all times to an effective synthetic support for spiritual realization. The rites of the pipe express sacrifice and purification; they affirm the integration of the individual within the macrocosm, and they lead finally to the realization of unity, prefigured by the totality of the grains of tobacco becoming one with the fire of the Great Spirit.

There may be discerned in these spiritual ways of purification a pattern for which parallels may be found in virtually all the legitimate methods of spiritual realization within the world's great religions. This universal pattern affirms the sequence first of purification, followed by an expansive process in the realization of totality, or the state of human perfection, leading finally to the ultimate possibility of contact and identity with the one transcendent supreme principle.

CONTACT: DYNAMICS OF THE ACCULTURATION PROCESS

Is it possible today for small minority groups within the United States, or anywhere for that matter, to retain the integrity of cultural patterns and spiritual ways similar to those just described—ways rooted in traditions of primordial origin which had their essential supports in a world of nature still virgin and unscarred by the hand of any human being?

All the forces of historical contact between the American Indian and the materially dominant Euro-American civilization seem to be totally against the possibility of any traditional continuity for the Indian. The power of alien forces and the inevitable disruption of life-ways that has ensued must not be minimized. The people's subsistence base, the bison, was brought to near extinction through commercial exploitation combined with an avowed policy of extermination by the United States Army. Freedom of movement was restricted by force to reservations often arbitrarily chosen.

Governing techniques based on the accumulated wisdom of the elders were replaced by an imposed bureaucratic system, which could never, even if it wished, understand the real problems of the people under its charge. In accord with the Euro-American concept of ownership, the random distribution of parcels of land on the basis of individual family units shattered the cohesive unity of the Indian's own larger consanguineous groupings, and the prohibition of plural marriages disrupted the immediate family units. School systems were imposed that had as their avowed goals the suppression and eventual elimination of traditional values in order to hasten forcefully the process of total assimilation. This policy, with all too few exceptions, is still basic to today's school system on the reservation. Ill-conceived government attempts at economic rehabilitation have ended again and again in total failure largely due to the fact that agriculture, then identified by white people with civilization, was a practice contradictory to all Indian values, which held the earth as sacred and inviolate and not to be torn up with a plow. Among the most difficult trials, however, were the hostile attitudes toward the Indian's religious practices. Sacrificial elements of the Sun Dance were prohibited, as were the rites held for the departing souls of the dead, and it is well known how participation in the much-misunderstood Ghost Dance ended in the infamous massacre of Wounded Knee in 1890.

This series of traumatic shocks received by the Indian is obviously not just the inevitable result of straightforward military defeats, as devastating as these were, but rather the tragic drama of two cultures in conflict, each representing to the other diametrically opposed values on every possible level and in all domains. Such conflict between cultures was undoubtedly intensified by the fact that those segments of Euro-American society with which the Indian had the most contact were, with few exceptions, probably the least enlightened carriers of the more positive facets of "civilization." With the exception of some Christian missionaries of "good heart," the Indians found no segment of American society with which they could identify themselves.

After more than a century of this bitter confrontation with accompanying disruptions in social, economic, political, and religious life, it is difficult to understand how the people have survived at all. Yet the Plains Indians, as well as other groups, have survived with tenacity and even vitality that certain rites and ceremonies are actually undergoing renewed affirmation. Much to the surprise of the social scientists and the Bureau of Indian Affairs itself, the "vanishing American" has somehow not vanished at all. It had been incorrectly assumed, among other factors, that just as so many European immigrants had readily assimilated into the great American "melting pot," so too would the Indian. There was obviously a failure to take into account the tremendous differences between the European and the American Indian. The result of this new awareness, on the part of anthropologists at least, has led to a growing number of hypotheses to explain the phenomenon of the tenacity of traditional values and cultures.

One such hypothesis has pointed to the isolation of the reservations. This is undoubtedly an important factor, yet it must be recalled that for certain groups—the Mohawk, for example, who construct skyscrapers in New York City—close and frequent contact has not resulted in the total abandonment of ancient values. The sustaining power of culture-bearing indigenous languages has been reflected in the literature; certainly it has been well understood by the reservation school systems, which, at one time, often forbid children, under threat of punishment, to speak their own native language.

It has been suggested, with reason, that the policies of forced or "directed" acculturation to which all Indian groups have been subjected lead to violent reactions that reject change and reaffirm traditionalism. A converse possibility neglected by the specialists has been the role of the half-informed, usually sentimental "Indian lovers," the "do-gooders," who would preserve certain of the "more noble" Indian values while incorporating such modern innovations as housing and hygiene. Paradoxically, these seemingly sympathetic approaches may be far more corrosive to traditional values than the uncompromising ethnocentric attitudes of those who insist on total assimilation, by force if necessary.

Among the vast array of forces that work for the persistence of traditional values is the often neglected psychological factor of the inherent stability of the basic personality structure, which acts as a selective screen in processes of change. A dimension central to this complex question, but inaccessible to the quantitative experiential tools of either cultural anthropology or psychology, is the qualitative power of metaphysical, or cosmological, principles and the degree to which these become virtual or effective within the individual substance through participation in traditional rites and spiritual methods. Related to this entire question of the quality of personality is the fact that where Indians are still able to live in an area of as-yet-unspoiled nature, potentially they have access to a vast array of transcendent values. For this potential source to become virtual, however, the Indian must still possess, to a certain degree at least, the traditional metaphysic of nature. Where this metaphysic is still understood, and can be directly related to the supporting forms of the natural world, the Indian has here perhaps the strongest ally in preserving essential values. It is also in this metaphysic of nature that we find the Indian's most valuable message for the contemporary world.

A final factor relating to the persistence of values is crucial today to a multitude of problems deriving from attitudes in America toward minority groups of various ethnic backgrounds. Euro-American racial attitudes have historically so tended to devaluate physical types of other cultural traditions that these peoples generally have been relegated to positions of inferior status in the larger society. In thus being denied the possibility of social or cultural mobility, many of these groups have tended to seek cohesion and identity through reaffirmation of their own traditional values. The resulting low index of intermarriage between these minority groups and the dominant majority has also tended to slow acculturation. (This situation, incidentally, has not occurred in Mexico, where positive valuation has been given to the Indian heritage.) Among the ramifications of negative racist attitudes is that many Indians who do attempt to assimilate into segments of Euro-American culture tend to undergo a cycle of progressive disenchantment, a process often hastened by the slum conditions of cities or by participation in foreign wars. When such persons then attempt to reintegrate themselves into their own traditional societies they often serve as powerful agents for the preservation of traditional values.

CONTEMPORARY ASSESSMENT
Several centuries of direct contact of the diverse Plains Indian groups with Euro-Americans has resulted in such a broad spectrum of adjustments, conservative reactions, or total changes that it is obviously impossible to make valid generalizations in terms of the contemporary persistence of values. Within this spectrum of multiple possibilities there are examples, across groups as well as within particular groups, of near-total retention of traditional values at the one end of the scale to near-total assimilation at the other end. The vast majority of groups or individuals, however, probably lie in the mid-range and generally

represent a more or less synthetic reassemblage of Indian and Euro-American values, always with the retention, however, of a remarkable degree of traditional Indianness.

Available data indicate that concordant with a high degree of traditional persistence a culture generally has cohesiveness and direction and affords personal dignity. Assimilation, on the contrary, can often represent acculturation into the lowest and least enlightened segments of Euro-American society. This can be the first step leading to extreme cultural disintegration, producing the dangerous phenomenon of a de-cultured people living precariously in a vacuum, unable to identify either with Indianness or with any of the Euro-American values.

In viewing the degree of cultural wreckage strewn today across the prairies, it is impressive and hopeful that so many of the core indigenous values, with their supporting rites, are generally persisting among most Plains groups. In spite of the virtual disappearance of a host of minor rites, still being practiced are the rites of purification, the Sun Dance, the spiritual retreat, and the rites of the sacred pipe. Sacred arrows, the original sacred pipe, and sacred bundles in general are still being kept with reverence and respect, even though some of the spiritual meanings of these forms may have been lost. One of the most notable aspects of these examples of traditional tenacity is the fact that those who today affirm these forms and values are not necessarily just the "long hairs," the old men; there is a growing interest and participation on the part of the younger generations as well.

An outstanding example of the contemporary process of reaffirmation is the increasing participation throughout the Plains in the Sun Dance. Among the complex factors contributing to this revitalization, which cannot be explained here in detail, is the example and stimulus afforded by a dynamic series of interpersonal and intercultural relationships between the Crow Indians of Montana and the Shoshone of Wyoming. The renewed interest among the younger generations may be partly because the youths have not been able to find channels in white society for the expression of specific needs, personal qualities, or virtues, which had always been central, and which still are relevant, to the indigenous cultures. Public display of personal courage, sacrifice, and generosity, for example, are key Indian themes dramatically affirmed in the context of the Sun Dance.

Although the three- or four-day total fast required in the Sun Dance is still observed, the self-torture features have not been publicly participated in since the government prohibitions of 1890. Such tortures, however, are still engaged in secretly by certain individuals.

Also little known to outside groups is the fact that the spiritual retreat is frequently used today not only by the old, but also by the young. It is evident, although it has not been specifically mentioned, that crucial to the spiritual ways that have been mentioned is the presence of the shaman or medicine man. Judging partly from the frequency and popularity of *Yuwipi* rites, which allow for the ritual demonstration of shamanistic powers, it appears that shamanism still plays a meaningful role among the people and that it continues to have mechanisms for the transmission of power. The high personal quality and magnetism of many of these people are very strong contributing factors to the holding power of traditional values.

The true nature of a growing number of pan-Indian movements, or what I call the powwow syndrome, still remains questionable, for the stimulus behind many of the movements is a reaction to Euro-American attitudes toward ethnic minorities. In being rejected the Indian affirms his or her Indianness, yet in doing this often seeks to identify with the white person's image of what an Indian is—or should be. The result is a complex of heterogeneous forms and practices that have popular appeal and commercial advantage, but that risk sacrificing true spiritual content. The extraordinary growth of the new Black Elk Sweat Lodge Organization, with membership cards and all, is undoubtedly a good example of this double-edged phenomenon of pan-Indianism.

Will educational policy, which for so long has been dictated to the Indian, honor and support indigenous values and life-ways so that the young may grow with a rightful pride in their own heritage? Or must the schools continue in their efforts toward total assimilation, thus denying Indians their birthright and robbing the larger American culture of the possibility of a spiritual enrichment that present crises indicate is so desperately needed?

Cannot Indian lands be allowed to remain inviolate, so that a unique religious heritage may continue to retain its supports in a world of sacred natural forms? Or must policies for rapid termination of protective mechanisms continue so that remaining Indian-held lands will melt away under the pressures of often unscrupulous commercial interests?

But above all, and crucial to these and many other questions: Can it not be affirmed that all peoples, regardless of skin color, ethnic background, or religious affiliation, are rightful members of one family of humankind? Should not differences of appearance, culture, or religion be affirmed as valid and even necessary expressions of a greater Reality, so that they may contribute to a richer world? Any alternative cannot but lead to drab mediocrity and ultimate chaos.

Whatever the outcome, we might well heed the words attributed to a great Indian after whom one of our cities was named, Seattle.

> We are two distinct races with separate origins and separate destinies. To us the ashes of our ancestors are sacred and their resting place is hallowed ground. You wander far from the graves of your ancestors and seemingly without regret. . . .
>
> But why should I mourn at the untimely fate of my people? Tribe follows tribe and nation follows nation, and regret is useless. . . .
>
> But when the last Red man shall have become a myth among the White man . . . when your children's children think themselves alone in the field . . . or in the silence of the pathless woods, they will not be alone . . . your hands will throng with the returning hosts that once filled them and still love this beautiful land. The White man will never be alone.
>
> Let him be just and deal kindly with my people for the dead are not powerless. Dead—I say? There is no death. Only a change of worlds.[1]

[1] Frank Waters, "Two Views of Nature: White and Indian," *The South Dakota Review*, May 1964, pp. 28-29.

CHAPTER 5

CONTEMPLATION THROUGH ACTION

What we refer to as religion cannot, in the case of the American Indian, be separated from the forms and dynamics of everyday life, or from almost any facet of the total culture; nor, as we shall see more clearly, may there be separation from the phenomena of the natural environment. This situation is typical of religious traditions that still remain close to their primal origins and have subsisted at a technological level that does not allow alienation from the environment. One cannot, therefore, find in these cultures the kinds of systematic theological structures that have become central to most of the historical religions. We could distill out and formulate such structures, since they are latently there, but the people themselves do not overtly make such abstractions from life and experienced reality. Religious concepts and values are given substance through the direct visual or pictorial image and through the symbol, which includes the auditory word or echo, all of which have reference always to the forms, forces, and voices of nature.

A further barrier to understanding primitive traditions may be that within the context of the historical and generally monotheistic religions, only two mutually exclusive theistic possibilities seem to be affirmed. That is, religions are either monotheistic or polytheistic, and generally monotheism has been taken as the sign of advancement in civilization. Primitive religions, however, and specifically here the American Indian traditions, do not fit into either one of these categories. Rather, these traditions represent a form of theism wherein concepts of both monotheism and polytheism intermingle and fuse without being confused. Among the western Lakota and eastern Dakota of the Plains, for example, the term *Wakan-Tanka*, Great Mysterious, is an all-inclusive concept that refers both to a Supreme Being and to the totality of all gods or spirits or powers of creation. Such conceptualizations embracing both unity and diversity are typical of the polysynthetic nature of the languages of these peoples, and thus of their modes of conceptualization and cognitive orientations. Black Elk was able to affirm: "*Wakan-Tanka*, you are everything, and yet above everything." Abundant recorded materials make it evident beyond any doubt that this type of ultimate affirmation of a Supreme Being was held before the coming of white people and Christian missionaries, not only among the Lakota, but among most, if not all, American Indian peoples. The contemporary Navajo artist Carl Gorman, speaking from a culture very different from that of the Plains people, has recently written:

> It has been said by some researchers into Navajo religion, that we have no Supreme God, because He is not named. That is not so. The Supreme Being is not named because He is unknowable. He is simply the Unknown Power. We worship him through His Creation. We feel too insignificant to approach directly in prayer that Great Power that is incomprehensible to man. Nature feeds our soul's inspiration and so we approach Him through that part of Him which is close to us and within the reach of human understanding. We believe that this great unknown power is everywhere in His creation. The various forms of creation have some of this spirit within them. . . . As every form has some of the intelligent spirit of the Creator, we cannot but reverence all parts of the creation.[1]

The implications of this type of primitive religion are far reaching and have relevance to certain theological and existential problems of historical religions. The problem that particularly concerns us here is the lack today within the historical religions of an adequate metaphysic of nature. Such a metaphysic was certainly present in the origins of the Judeo-Christian tradition, but is now being forgotten. Neglect has left the way open, as we currently have seen in an abundance of tragic examples, for abuses of the natural environment.

Unlike the conceptual categories of Western culture, American Indian traditions generally do not fragment experience into mutually exclusive dichotomies, but tend rather to stress modes of interrelatedness across categories of meaning, never losing sight of an ultimate wholeness. Our animate-inanimate dichotomy, or our categories of animal, vegetable, and mineral, for example, have no meaning for the Indian, who sees that all that exists is animate, each form in its own special way, so that even rocks have a life of their own and are believed to be able to talk under certain conditions. Creatures we relegate to the category "animal" or "bird" and consider inferior to humans, the Indian refers to as "peoples" who, in a sense, have a recognized superiority to humans. It is generally believed that in the order of creation

---

[1] Carl N. Gorman, "Navajo Vision of Earth and Man," *The Indian Historian*, Winter 1973.

animals were here before humans, and in these cultures what is anterior in time has a certain superiority over that which comes later. (It is this belief that accounts for the enormous respect shown to the aged among Native American peoples.)

This mode of interrelatedness may be seen in the Lakota's discernment of a certain unity underlying that which we perceive generally as very different kinds of beings or phenomena. For example, spiders, elks, bisons, birds, flying insects, and even cottonwood trees have a unifying element, for all these manifest certain relationships to the wind or breath.[2] There is, in fact, a qualitative and comprehensive science of the winds among these peoples that has as its ultimate unifying principle the understanding that as the wind moves or exerts power over the forms of nature and yet in itself is unseen, so it is with the Great Mysterious whose unseen presence gives life and movement to all that is. Such modes of conceptualization are often conveyed through mythical expressions that anthropomorphize the four winds, naming them as brothers identified with the four directions of space, each with his own particular qualities or forces; ultimately the four brothers are seen to be the sons of a single named father figure. There are, of course, other members of this particular family of unlikely associates unified by the wind or breath as principle. Always, however, such configurations are expressed in terms of directly experienced natural phenomena.

The generally understood meaning of the symbol—as a form that stands for or points to, something other than the particular form or expression—is incomprehensible to the Indian. To the Indian's cognitive orientation, meanings generally are intuitively sensed and not secondarily interpreted through analysis; there tends to be a unity between form and idea or content. Here the "symbol" *is*, in a sense, that to which it refers. The tree at the center of the Sun Dance lodge does not just represent the axis of the world, but *is* that axis and *is* the center of the world. The eagle is not a symbol of the sun, but *is* the sun in a certain sense; and similarly, the sun is not a symbol of the Creative Principle, but *is* that Principle as manifested in the sun. When a Navajo singer executes a sand painting of one of the gods, or *Yei*, the painting

---

[2] Spiders, newly hatched, are carried on long filaments by the winds; the mysterious whistling call of the bull elk, through the use of his breath, attracts the cows to him; a bison cow, breathing over her calf in a cold winter, can enclose the young animal in a protective film-like sac; birds and insects utilize and exercise control over the winds with their wings; and through the winds a cottonwood tree in season sends out its seeds wrapped in "cotton."

does not represent the god; the god is really present there and radiates toward all participants at the ceremony its particular grace or power.

It is not that these concepts of the symbol, or of mythic time, are in real contrast to the same concepts of the historical religions. Generally, the contrast is rather between traditional people and modern people who attempt to live in a desacralized world and who govern their lives through the artificial segments of clock-time, through linear rather than circular projections. American Indian traditions speak to us with special force today partly because these traditions, and of course other "exotic" outside traditions, appear to be more total and less hypocritical. They seem to represent a gratifyingly integrated and intense participation across a very wide spectrum of experiences. Aspects of the Indian's world do not become sacralized only within the context of special liturgical occasions (although obviously there are special occasions where intensity is generated), but rather, as is generally the case with peoples close to their primal sources, the total world of experience is seen as being infused with the sacred.

Given the above considerations, it should now be clear that if we are to speak with precision about modes of contemplation and action for American Indians, it will be necessary to examine in detail, and through more specific examples, their modes of understanding their natural environment, and the quality of their structured relationships to specific forms.

With the American Indians we are dealing ultimately with a quality of culture wherein action and contemplation are interrelated and integrated. Or, if we wish to make a sharper distinction between meditation and contemplation, it may be said that special rituals and ceremonials, as well as the routines of everyday life, constitute meditative acts that open, to the exceptional person at least, possibilities for pure contemplation. A hunter, for example, is not just participating in a purely mechanical subsistence activity, but is engaged in a complex of meditative acts, all of which—whether preparatory prayer and purification, pursuit of the quarry, or the sacramental manner by which the animal is slain and subsequently treated—are infused with the sacred. Black Elk described the act of hunting as being—not representing—life's quest for ultimate truth. Hunting is a quest, he insisted, that requires preparatory prayer and sacrificial purification; the diligently followed tracks are signs or intimations of the goal, and final contact or identity with the quarry is the realization of Truth, the ultimate goal of life. Similar examples of hunting as a meditative rite could be presented from the southwestern peoples, and Frank Speck has found the same attitudes among the Naskapi hunters of the Labrador peninsula.

In their visual art forms, there is no separation between the created form of whatever medium, and the message or power this form bears and transmits. It may be the case that the powers of certain forms must become activated through rite, song, or prayer, yet the power is always latently present in the created design or object. Across the great variety of such created works there cannot, in the first place, be found that occidental distinction between art and craft, for in a primal as in any normal society it would be inconceivable to separate art from life, or the practical from the beautiful.[3]

The natural materials used by the American Indians were always respected in the fullness of their context, that is, as being produced from the sacred substances and generative forces of the earth. "Material" resources were thus gathered with prayer, song, and sacrifice, or even in holy pilgrimage with appropriate formal rites and ceremonies. Every being and natural substance had a life and power of its own that was to be respected, for these powers could be transmitted to humans. The hunting of animals was therefore a ritual activity in which the hunted offered up its being to the hunter. Food and hides and all parts of the animal were therefore understood to partake of this sacrificial act, and of the sacred power of the particular animal. In making objects for special ritual use it was inappropriate even to puncture the hide of the animal with arrow or bullet; certain animals such as the deer or antelope were slain by being run down on foot and then ritually suffocated, so that the sacred life breath of the animal would be contained within its being. If clothing was to be made, care would be taken to honor the animal by not cutting or trimming the hide, but to leave it as if it were still the outer clothing of the being who originally wore it. In wearing such a garment or robe a person would thus partake of the spiritual qualities or powers latent in the particular animal. For in this vision all beings and resources of creation were understood to manifest

[3] One of the great tragedies in the history of world art is that the sacred language of American Indian art forms has been subjected to occidental criteria. Under such impoverished vision museums have tended to exhibit Indian "craft items" as quaint examples of a peoples' "material culture," useful for classifying culture areas, or perhaps for tracing diffusion routes, but never presented as true art. In spite of signs of new awareness on the part of some museum curators and art historians, museums and art books continue to present American Indian arts and crafts as *things*, of aesthetic quality perhaps, but extracted out of the ritual and ceremonial context which is essential to full understanding as this was available to those who created, used, and lived with such forms.

qualitatively differentiated powers that could be assimilated by man or woman.

All images that were painted or depicted with natural materials were experienced as immediate presences bearing and radiating powers specific to both the form depicted and to the materials used. Quasi-naturalistic representation may have been used for special circumstances, but abstract representation was more prevalent, for in just a single aspect of a depicted being—in the paw of a grizzly bear or in a painted image of an elk track—the full force of the entire being was presented and experienced. In objects of special power, such as the painted hide shields of the Plains Indian, the depicted images were revealed in visions or dreams received through fasting or in retreat, and their protective functions could only become operative through the use of prayer, sacred song, or ritual acts. A style of painting of shamanic origin, diffused across many areas of the Americas, presents animal forms as if they were transparent. Through elegant abstract treatment, the inner vital and generative organs are depicted on the surface of the being, allowing the viewer to penetrate into the most interior and sacred realm. These widespread representations reveal the presiding American Indian vision of creation and process wherein the forms of existence are experienced as the outer shell of interior and spiritual realities.

Stone "effigy" pipes, which are widely diffused in the Americas—and in museums—may be grand examples of aesthetically pleasing and powerful sculpture, but again their full efficacy and power are in the dynamics of their ritual use. When a person smokes, the flow of breath is drawn from the source of life in the central fire-containing bowl, and when the bowl is carved with animal beings facing the one who smokes, a circular relationship, by means of visual image and shared breath, is established. This is typical of almost all American Indian art forms, which express through a multitude of means both relationship and identity. When a vessel is molded from moist clay, relationship with the creative force of the earth is established, the maker becomes Creator, and the completed vessel is a living being, both alive and containing life. This is why the Mimbres painted bowls of southwest burials are found with holes in the bottom, for in this manner, and appropriate to the occasion, the life of the vessel is ritually killed.

Similar kinds of meditative or contemplative attitudes are present over a vast range of other activities. The southwestern Pima or Papago, or any of the basket-making peoples, perceived in their acts of gathering grasses and vegetable dyes, and in the weaving process itself, the ritual recapitulation of the total process of creation. The completed basket is the universe in an image; and in the manufacturing process the woman actually plays the part of the Creator. Similarly, in establishing the dynamic interrelationship between the vertical warp and the horizontal weft, the Navajo blanket weaver participates in acts that imitate the creation of the universe itself. As indicated above, it may be that the practitioner of such kinds of traditional crafts will not be able to consciously analyze or interpret such "symbolism"; nevertheless, through the force of myth and oral traditions, such values are intuitively sensed and participated in with the total being and not just with the mind.

When a Plains Indian woman decorates a robe with porcupine quills, she is not just involved in making a useful, aesthetically pleasing object. As a member of a women's quillwork "guild" she is obliged to fast and pray before commencing her work, and she must retain a contemplative attitude as she works with the brightly dyed quills. Because of the formal and initiatory nature of the quillworker's guild, the woman will probably be aware of the identity between the porcupine and the sun, and that the sun is a manifestation of the Creative Principle. The quills she lays on in geometrical patterns established by tradition are really rays of the sun and thus eminently sacred. The quillworker has, as it were, trapped the sun, understood as a spiritual principle, upon a garment now of utilitarian, aesthetic, and spiritual value. These values are real and functional both to the maker and to the wearer of the garment. Neither art nor what we call religion are divorced from each other or from life.

Similar modes of spiritual conceptualization are involved in the making of dwellings and ceremonial structures: in the tipi, the domed sweat lodge, the Sun Dance lodge of the Plains, the round or octagonal hogan of the Navajo, the wickiup of the Apache, and the long houses of woodland peoples such as the Iroquois or Menomomini. All these dwellings are created in imitation of the process of the creation of the world itself, and are perceived as sacred. They thus serve as supports for meditation. Living with such forms makes it almost impossible to forget the transcendent dimension of life.

A multitude of meditative acts with their supporting forms could be identified across the great diversity of cultures and in relation to a vast range of expressions and activities. A rich array of major rites and ceremonies of special intensity could similarly be presented for many groups, such as the synthetic and profound spiritual meanings expressed in the rites of the sacred pipe; the elaborate four-day communal and sacrificial rites of the Sun Dance of the Plains Indians; the seven- or nine-day Navajo ceremonies for reestablishing the health of a person who has become ill through being in a state of disharmony with the universe; and the complex initiatory rites, such as the *Medewewin*, of many of the woodland peoples. One additional mode of participation in the sacred is the foundation of all that has been presented above, and it brings us perhaps closest to the heart of these cultures. I am referring to the retreat or "vision quest."

Through the vision quest, participated in with physical sacrifice and the utmost humility, the individual is opened in the most direct manner to contact with the spiritual essences underlying the forms of the manifested world. In the states achieved at this level, meditation may be surpassed by contemplation. Thus Black Elk has said that the greatest power in the retreat is contact with silence, "for is not silence the very voice of the Great Spirit?" In certain cultures the retreat is initiatory in character for young men or occasionally for young women, who seek spiritual sanction for a new and sacred name; in the arctic, or among some southwestern peoples, this retreat is participated in only by those who seek the necessary spiritual power for becoming special religious practitioners, a shaman, a medicine man, or a "singer," the term used by the Navajo and the Apache. Among many groups the retreat was specifically associated with the quest for a guardian spirit, although this is not as general a phenomenon as the vision quest itself. Among the Plains people the vision quest was most intensely developed; it was an activity that was expected of every young man, and frequently of every young woman, participated in not just once at a certain time in his or her life, but indeed with frequency throughout the life of the individual. No one in these societies, it was believed, could have success in any of the activities of the culture without the unique spiritual power received through the quest.

The minimal formal elements of the retreat involved the guidance of a spiritual mentor, preliminary rites of purification, the seeking out of an isolated place, usually on a mountain top, and the observance of a total fast. At the place of the retreat, special patterns for the participant's actions, and often special forms of prayer, were indicated to the supplicant by the mentor. Essentially, the person was to be exposed, normally for four days and nights, to the elements and to the forms and forces of nature; he or she should be attentive to whatever might appear, no matter how insignificant the being or phenomenon might seem to be. If a dream should come to the participant while asleep, this too could be of import. Although the dream was considered to be of lesser power, or as auxiliary to the true vision, nevertheless the person should be attentive to such experiences and should be able to relate them to the guide, who might explain their spiritual implications. Indeed, many of Black Elk's dreams seemed to be very close to the vision experience. I recall one such power dream that he recounted to me: "I was taken away from this world into a vast tipi, which seemed to be as large as the world itself, and painted on the inside were every kind of four-legged being, winged being, and all the crawling peoples. These peoples who were there in that lodge, they talked to me, much as I am talking to you."

Not all who sought, or "lamented," for a vision received the experience. When the experience did come, however, it was in the form of some being, a bird or animal, or of the powers and phenomena of the natural world. Usually the being spoke to the supplicant, giving a message revealing some aspect of wisdom which it manifested or possessed. The supplicant, it was believed, thus established an identity, not just with the form in itself, but with the spiritual essence of the form, which conveyed a specific quality of spiritual power. The gradation of such power was recognized in accord with the nature of the experience and the type of being that appeared. Frequently, the animal or bird might become the individual's guardian spirit, which would protect him or her in the events of life; it might instruct in specific virtues, or convey skills and qualities of special importance to the activities of the society. Spiritual powers could be accumulated through the frequency of such vision experiences, and thus always the great leaders of the community were persons who had received powers through many visions. Without the vision a person was considered to be a nobody and could be successful in nothing. Something of this power received by the individual was communicated to the people generally, not only through the special personality of the individual concerned, but the recipient was also required to publicly externalize the experience through a special dance, the sacred songs received, or through the paintings that he or she had made on the shield or garment. Also, to insure the continuing activation of the vision power within the individual, some part of the animal would be worn on his or her person or kept carefully wrapped in a special bundle. Occasionally such bundles could be acquired by others to whom a vision had never come, for it was believed that the spiritual power, once manifested to a particular person, was then operative in and by itself, so long as certain prescribed requirements for the keeping of the bundle were met.

In American Indian cultures the vision experience served in an especially forceful manner to render transparent to the individual some facet of the phenomenal world, revealing aspects of a spiritual world of greater reality underlying this world of appearances. In and through such qualities of experience, consciously or not those barriers are dissolved that have tended to set apart what is experienced as an "outer world"; the vision experience integrates and interrelates these "inner" and "outer" worlds into one. The beings, or whatever might be involved in the vision, serve as intermediaries revealing aspects of reality through which the ultimate reality of the Great Mysterious (*Wakan-Tanka*) may be contemplated, if not comprehended.

Understood in its total context, this type of religion, with its specific modes of spiritual realization, proceeds in a circular continuum through the domains of action, meditation, and contemplation, leading back again to action. The mysteries of the natural world provide all the spiritual means.

> We should understand well that all things are the works of the Great Spirit. We should know that He is within all things: the trees, the grasses, the rivers, the mountains, and the four-legged animals, and the winged peoples; and even more important, we should understand that He is also above all these things and peoples. When we do understand all this deeply in our hearts, then we will fear, and love, and know the Great Spirit, and then we will be and act and live as He intends.[4]

---

[4] Black Elk, quoted in *The Sacred Pipe*, p. xx.

CHAPTER 6

THE IMMEDIACY OF
MYTHOLOGICAL MESSAGE

"If we knew and understood fairytales—and by extension the myth—we would not need the scriptures." This insight of profound implication by G. K. Chesterton is indicative of a change from previous centuries when myth was synonymous with fable, fiction, and poetic invention—an account that was interesting and often amusing, but nevertheless always untrue, a connotation that "myth" still conveys in the popular language of today.

Writing of the Huron in the seventh century, Père Raguenau summarizes well the generally accepted and often repeated opinions of that era: "To speak truly, all the nations of those countries have received from their ancestors no knowledge of a God; and, before we set foot here, all that was related about the creation of the world consisted of nothing but myths" (*Relation*, 1647-48).

Due to a growing number of more enlightened and objective contemporary scholars, those of us who live outside of oral mythic traditions have come closer to an understanding of the realities and truths of mythic statements as understood by peoples who still live by their sacred traditions. Such peoples find in their myths, and oral traditions generally, models for human behavior, statements told and ritually enacted that tell of the origins and ultimate realities of existence, accounts and acts that define the sacred and make it immediate in all its mysterious modes of operation. In the spirit of this new understanding the great oriental scholar, Ananda Coomaraswamy, has written:

> The Myth [is] the penultimate truth, of which all experience is the temporal reflection. The mythical narrative is of timeless and placeless validity, true nowever and everywhere. . . . Myth embodies the nearest approach to absolute truth that can be stated in words.[1]

Or elsewhere, "Myth is to history as Universal is to particular."

---

[1] Ananda Coomaraswamy, *Hinduism and Buddhism* (Westport, Connecticut: Greenwood Press), p. 6; p. 33, note 21.

From this perspective we will examine selected aspects of the mythologies of Native American peoples that relate to what may be called the immediacy of mythological message. There are other possible orientations and uses of the myth, such as the functionalist and structuralist approaches of the contemporary anthropological sciences. These approaches often tend to be poverty-stricken exercises, but they may hold value where they serve to clarify and elucidate the sacred dimensions of the mythic statement or accompanying ritual act as understood and lived by the Native American peoples themselves.

There are obviously great diversities in the mythologies held and lived by Native American peoples, and thus in the cosmologies, world views, and religious and ritual expressions, all of which have their origin and reinforcement in the myth. Central to this rich diversity, however, is a common perspective that particularly deserves our attention: a concept of time manifest in all real myths and continually expressed in profound ritual enactments of mythic themes and sacred events—time outside of time, that is, the sacred time of the *hierophany* of the now. The recitation of a myth defining creation, for example, is not experienced in terms of an event of linear time past, but rather of a happening of eternal reality, true and real now and forever, a time on the "knife edge between the past and the future."

To illustrate this immediacy of mythological message as it occurs across the Native Americans' experience, I have selected from an enormous range of possibilities the myths of three groups who are distinct linguistically, culturally, and geographically. The Algonquin "Earth-Diver" myth, because of its profound expression of a form of theism typically and pervasively experienced by many Native American peoples, particularly expresses the perspective of an immediacy of experience. Three interrelated selections from translations of Navajo creation myths express immediacy in other modes, specifically through the perspective of individual identification. Portions of a northern Washington Kathlamet Chinook text, known as "The Sun's Myth," recorded in 1891 by Franz Boas from Charles Cultee, makes a perennial statement concerning the nature of the human soul, of desire and pride, of punishment and subsequent reconciliation, set in the context of the changing events of time. Finally, I wish to stress that the immediacy of the message is conveyed through the use and understanding of language, through the rich and creative variety of means by which myths, and oral traditions generally, are transmitted by the teller.

The "Earth-Diver" myth of the Algonquin peoples of the eastern Woodlands and the Plains is well known in several of its many versions.

The creation of land where there is only water takes place not out of nothingness, but within the perspective of cyclical process, for land was there before this particular deluge, and thus is now underneath the waters and must be recovered. Further, an Earth-Maker figure, Manabush or Nanabozo, the Great Hare among the central Algonquins, or Old Man (*Napi*) among the western Algonquins, is already there upon these waters; in some versions he is holding the peoples' most sacred pipe, often identified with creation and creative power, as among the Algonquin-speaking Arapaho.[2] Indeed, all the aquatic birds and animals are there with Earth Maker, who instructs them to dive down under the waters to find even a small grain of earth from which new land may be made. Typically, the otter, beaver, and mink take turns diving under the waters, each being unsuccessful in the mission. After much suspense in the telling of the account, it is always the fourth being, most often the muskrat, who finally surfaces, after four days underwater, with a little bit of earth on his paws.[3] Often this earth is placed upon the back of a turtle, as among the southern Ontario Ojibwa, where the turtle itself represents, or is, the earth as well as fertility. Through the agency of breath Earth Maker then fashions and enlarges the earth, establishing its features and contours until it is again a suitable habitation for all the beings of water and land, finally including human beings.

The key themes in this grand account illustrate a message of immediacy. First, creation here occurs not just once out of nothingness in linear time past, but is an event ever occurring and recurring in cyclical fashion, just as the observable cycle of days or seasons speak of death and rebirth. As with each form of creation, the mystery of this creative cycle of birth, life, death, and life is immediately and continually manifest to one who is attentive. Second, the myth informs us that certain beings, already created, participate and cooperate with the Creator Figure in the act of creation. This again shifts the orientation away from creation understood as a single event of time past, to the reality of those immediately experienced processes of creation ever happening and observable through all the multiple forms and forces of creation.

There are those who might insist that such accounts of a Creator cooperating with creation compromise a more ultimate belief in a Su-

---

[2] Cf. John G. Carter, "The Northern Arapaho Flat Pipe," *Bureau of American Ethnology,* Bulletin 119, 1938.

[3] One trait of the muskrat, observed by the people, is to build its house in the water out of mud; the house is dome-shaped and circular as is the earth.

preme Principle transcendent to all creation. Closer examination of Algonquin beliefs reveals however, that this is not the case. Among the Blackfeet, for example, it was Old Man (*Napi*) who requested the animals' cooperation in creating. *Napi*, however, may refer to many perspectives within creation; he is a trickster and bringer of important cultural forms, and his is also a name for the sun understood in its creative role;[4] but on a more ultimate level, it is believed, this visible sun derives its creative power from an invisible source transcendent to the realm of manifestation and is thus an ultimate Principle. This ultimate Principle is referred to by the Algonquin Ojibwa as *Kitchi Manitou*, usually translated as Great Spirit, as distinct from *manitou*, which refers to one of a number of qualitatively differentiated spirit beings or powers. There is a splendid Winnebago account that may serve to clarify this question.

A young man blackened his face and fasted in retreat for four days, for he sought to dream of nothing less than the Earth Maker. "He persevered until he had dreamed of everything in the whole world, but he never saw Ma-o-na," the Earth Maker. Even though the Spirits told him that he *had* dreamed of Ma-o-na because he had dreamed of all his works, the young man still was not satisfied. Finally the youth was given to understand the mystery that Ma-o-na in Himself cannot be seen, and yet at the same time all the visible and experienced forms and forces of creation that the youth had dreamed of are no other than Ma-o-na, so therefore he himself is no other than that.[5]

Formulated in such Native American mythologies are beliefs that serve as a profound and powerful response to the Judeo-Christian form of theism, which tends to insist on monotheism understood in an exclusive sense. Such belief, at least at a certain level of understanding, tends to become excessively remote from the mysteries of observable nature in all her modes of operation. Certainly, students concerned with problems of environmental abuse and degradation have pointed to the ramifications of this possibility. No less than Arnold Toynbee, that great historian of Western religions and civilization, wrote the following in *The New York Times* on September 16, 1973—one of his last pieces of writing before his death.

---

[4] George Bird Grinnell, "The Blackfoot Genesis," *Blackfoot Lodge Tales* (Lincoln, Nebraska: University of Nebraska Press, 1962).

[5] For the full account see Natalie Curtis, *The Indians' Book* (Harper & Brothers, 1907), pp. 262-263.

For premonotheistic man, nature was not just a treasure-trove of "natural resources." Nature was, for him, a goddess, "Mother Earth," and the vegetation that sprang from the earth's surface, the animals that roamed, like man himself, over the earth's surface, and the minerals hiding in the earth's hovels all partook of nature's divinity. The whole of his environment was divine. . . . My observation of the living religion of eastern Asia, and my book knowledge of the extinguished Greek and Roman religion, have made me aware of a startling and disturbing truth: that monotheism, as enunciated in the Book of Genesis, has removed the age-old restraint that was once placed on man's greed by his awe. Man's greedy impulse to exploit nature used to be held in check by his pious worship of nature. This primitive inhibition has been removed by the rise and spread of monotheism.

Native American beliefs in what has been called animism, so indirectly applauded by Toynbee but continually criticized by representatives of the historical monotheistic traditions, need to be understood in the larger contexts, as indicated by the above Algonquin myths, among many others. For neither animism, animatism, nor indeed expressions of polytheism, as they appear in Native American or any legitimate religious traditions, need exclude on other levels underlying concepts of monotheism or beliefs in an ultimate Principle, by whatever name this may be called. If animistic beliefs are understood as being ultimately attached to a unitary Principle, then a way is open to an especially profound realization as the mysteries of creative process, witnessed through every form and force of nature, are immediately experienced in the hierophany of the now.

Native American languages are joined to other sacred languages of the world in the sense that words are not conceived simply as symbols assigned arbitrarily to other units of meaning, as tends to be the case with our own English language. Rather, words in themselves are experienced in an immediate manner as units of power. Thus, to name a being or any element of creation is actually to make manifest the power or quality, soul or spirit, of that which is named. For this reason words and personal sacred names tend to be used carefully in Native American languages; one avoids using one's own or another person's sacred name, and especially, out of both respect and awe, the name of the deceased person. It is due to such a concept of language that N. Scott Momaday has titled his recent autobiography *The Names;* he tells us, "A man's life proceeds from his name, in the way that a river proceeds from its source."[6] He goes on to explain that his identity is achieved through his name which is one point in the river of the generations that preceded him.

Among the Athabaskan Navajo the words of their chantways have compulsive creative power; to name the *Yei*, for example—which we inadequately translate as "gods"—is to compel those who are named to be actually, immediately present. Similarly, as the visual counterpart to the audible, the sacred beings of the dry-paintings are present in their representations. Sacred curative powers are transmitted through word and form not just to the patient for whom the rites are performed; having been ritually drawn into a center, these powers eventually affect all life as they expand like ripples on the surface of the water when a pebble is dropped.

Against the background of these comments on the language of the Navajo, there follow brief excerpts from four separate Navajo chantway texts involving myths of creation. Although these are separate texts, they interrelate in a cumulative manner.

The first selection is a "sweathouse" song, for among the Navajo, as well as for other Native American peoples, the sweat lodge and its rites are associated with creation.

The earth has been laid down, the earth has been laid down
The earth has been laid down, it has been made.
The earth spirit has been laid down
It is covered over with the growing things, it has been laid down
The earth has been laid down, it has been made.
The sky has been set up, the sky has been set up
The sky has been set up, it has been made.
The mountains have been laid down, the mountains have been laid
* down*
The mountains have been laid down, they have been made.
The mountain spirits have been laid down
They are covered over with all the animals, they have been laid
* down*
The mountains have been laid down, they have been made.
The waters have been laid down, the waters have been laid down
The waters have been laid down, they have been made.
The water spirits have been laid down
They are covered over with the water pollen, they have been laid
* down*

[6] N. Scott Momaday, *The Names* (New York: Harper & Row, 1976).

The waters have been laid down, they have been made.
The clouds have been set up, the clouds have been set up
The clouds have been set up, the clouds have been made.

The establishment of the elements of the earth with their spirit counterparts is recounted here with that creative repetitive rhythmic force typical of Navajo chantways. The following chant extols the beauty, harmony, and peace of this earth in microcosmic anthropomorphic terms.

The Earth is beautiful
The Earth is beautiful
The Earth is beautiful
Below the East, the Earth, its face toward the East, the top of its head
  is beautiful
The soles of its feet, they are beautiful
Its legs, they are beautiful
Its body, it is beautiful
Its chest, it is beautiful
Its breath, it is beautiful
Its head-feather, it is beautiful
The Earth is beautiful.

With an earth of beauty created—and also the directions of space extolled in the remainder of the text, which has been omitted here—the following selection describes an ideal interrelationship between the human being and aspects of this created universe.

The Earth is looking at me; she is looking up at me
I am looking down on her
I am happy, she is looking at me
I am happy, I am looking at her.
The Sun is looking at me; he is looking down on me
I am looking up at him
I am happy, he is looking at me
I am happy, I am looking at him.
The Black Sky is looking at me; he is looking down on me
I am looking up at him
I am happy, he is looking at me
I am happy, I am looking at him.
The Moon is looking at me; he is looking down on me
I am looking up at him
I am happy, he is looking at me
I am happy, I am looking at him.

The North is looking at me; he is looking across at me
I am looking across at him
I am happy, he is looking at me
I am happy, I am looking at him.

In the final selection, which speaks with special and eloquent force to the perspective of immediacy with which we are particularly concerned, an identity is established between macrocosm and microcosm, between humankind and an earth of beauty, peace, and harmony—qualities expressed in the Navajo word *hozhoni.*

Hozhoni, hozhoni, hozhoni
Hozhoni, hozhoni, hozhoni
The Earth, its life am I, hozhoni, hozhoni
The Earth, its feet are my feet, hozhoni, hozhoni
The Earth, its legs are my legs, hozhoni, hozhoni
The Earth, its body is my body, hozhoni, hozhoni
The Earth, its thoughts are my thoughts, hozhoni, hozhoni
The Earth, its speech is my speech, hozhoni, hozhoni
The Earth, its down-feathers are my down-feathers, hozhoni, hozhoni
The sky, its life am I, hozhoni, hozhoni—
The mountains, their life am I—
Rain-mountain, its life am I—
Changing-Woman, her life am I—
The Sun, its life am I—
Talking God, his life am I—
House God, his life am I—
White corn, its life am I—
Yellow corn, its life am I—
The corn beetle, its life am I—
Hozhoni, hozhoni, hozhoni
Hozhoni, hozhoni, hozhoni.[7]

The perspective of immediacy in mythological message is illustrated in the following synopsis of a Kathlamet Chinook text known as the Sun's Myth, which deals with humankind's perennial pride, desire, and subsequent punishment and final reconciliation, a theme not unfamiliar to most of us.

[7] Recorded by Mary C. Wheelwright, from Hasteen Klah, *Navajo Creation Myth* (Santa Fe, New Mexico: Museum of Navajo Ceremonial Art, 1942; reprinted by ANTS, Inc., New York), pp. 136-137, 161, 149, 142.

Joseph E. Brown in Pine Ridge, South Dakota, 1948

Black Elk and wife, c. 1883

Black Elk, 1948

Mrs. Little Warrior, Little Warrior, and Black Elk, 1948

Little Warrior, 1948

John Trehero outside a Shoshone Sun Dance, 1940s

Thomas Yellowtail outside a Crow Sun Dance, 1979

Father Gall

Chief Dan Katchgonva, Hopi, Sun Clan, 1948

The chief of a village determines to take a journey to find the sun.[8]
After using up ten pairs of moccasins and ten pairs of leggings made
for him by his wife, he finally arrives at the very large house of the sun.
Entering, he meets a prepubescent girl and finds the house filled with
painted elkskin blankets, mountain goat blankets, and dressed buck-
skins decorated with dentalia shells; all the beautiful things prized by
these peoples of the Washington coast are itemized in great detail and
in repetitive manner. The girl informs the man that these things are
being saved for her maturity by her grandmother. Every evening the
grandmother returns to the house and hangs up a beautiful object that
is shining all over. The village chief finally takes the young girl and is
thus offered all the beautiful things hanging in the house. However, he
wishes only that one shining object, which the grandmother continually refuses to give to him. Finally he becomes homesick, and, wishing
to depart, insists with increasing persistence and anger on taking the
shining object with him. The grandmother, after many refusals and
warnings, finally hangs the shining object on him, and gives him a stone
axe. She tells him to depart and also that she had tried to love him. The
text of the myth continues:

> *He went out,*
> > *Now he went,*
> > > *he went home.*
> > > > *He did not see a land.*
> > > > > *He arrived near his uncle's town.*
> *Now that which he held shook,*
> > *Now that which he held said:*
> > > *"We two shall strike your town,*
> > > > *We two shall strike your town,"*
> > > > > *that which he held said.*
> *His reason became nothing,*
> > *He did it to his uncle's town,*
> > > *He crushed, crushed, crushed it,*
> > > > *he killed all the people.*
> *He recovered:*
> > *all those houses are crushed,*
> > > *His hands are full of blood.*
> *He thought,*

---

[8] The solar journey, in other myths, may express the opposite of this present version,
for a hero may travel to find the sun, or the house of the sun, which is his solar origin.
See, for example, *Where the Two Came to Their Father*, Bollingen Series I (Princeton,
New Jersey: Princeton University Press, 1969).

"O I am a fool!
      See, it is just like that, this thing;
         Why was I made to love it?"
            He tried in vain to wrench it off,
               and his flesh would be pulled.
Now again he went,
   and now he went a little while,
      now again his reason became nothing.
He arrived near another uncle's town.
   Now again it said,
"We two shall strike your town,
We two shall strike your town."
   He tried in vain to still it,
      it was never still.
      He tried in vain to throw it away,
         always his fingers closed.
Now again his reason became nothing,
   now again he did it to his uncle's town,
      he crushed it all.
He recovered:
   his uncle's town [is] nothing;
   all the people have become dead.
Now he cried.
In vain he tried in the fork of a tree,
   there in vain he would try squeezing it off,
      it would not at all come off,
         and his flesh would be pulled.
In vain he would try striking what he held on a stone,
   it would never be crushed.
Again he would go,
   he would arrive near another uncle's town.
      now again that which he held would shake:
         "We two shall strike your town,
         We two shall strike your town."
His reason would become nothing,
   he would do it to his uncle's town,
      crush, crush, crush, crush.
         He would destroy all his uncle's town,
            and he would destroy the people.
He would recover,
   he would cry out,
      he would grieve for his relatives.
He would try in vain diving in water,
   he would try in vain to wrench it off,
      and his flesh would be pulled.

> He would try in vain rolling in a thicket,
>> he would always try in vain striking what he held on a
>> stone.
> He would give up.
>> Now he would cry out.
> Again he would go,
>> Now again he would arrive at another town, an uncle's town.
>> Now again what he held would shake:
>>> "We two shall strike your town,
>>> We two shall strike your town."
> His reason would become nothing.
>> He would do it to the town,
>>> crush, crush, crush, crush,
>>>> and the people.
> He would recover.
>> All the people and the town [are] no more.
>> His hands and arms [are] only blood.
> He would become,
>> "Qa! qa! qa! qa!"
>> He would cry out.
> He would always try in vain striking stones,
>> what he held would not be crushed.
>>> He would always try in vain to throw away what he held,
>>> always his hands enclosed it.
> Again he would go,
>> Now next [is] his own town,
>> he would be near his own town.
>>> He would try to stand in vain,
>>> see, his feet would be pulled.
> His reason would become nothing,
>> he would do it to his town,
>> and he would destroy his relatives.
> He would recover.
>> His town [is] nothing.
>> The ground has become full of corpses.
> He would become,
>> "Qa! qa! qa! qa!"
>> he would cry out.
> He would try to bathe in vain,
>> he would try in vain to wrench off what he wore,
>> and his flesh would be pulled.
> Sometimes he would roll about on stones.
>> He would think,
>>> perhaps it will be broken apart.
> He would give up.

73

Now again he would cry out,
  and he wept.
He looked back,
  now she was standing there, that old woman.
"You,"
  she told him,
    "You.
  I try in vain to love you,
    I try in vain to love your relatives.
Why do you weep?
  It is you who choose,
    now you carried that blanket of mine."
Now she took it,
  she took off what he held.
Now she left him,
  she went home.
He stayed there.
  He went a little distance.
    There he built a house, a small house.[9]

The strength of this account of a perennial condition of the human soul is intensified and made all the more immediate for those who told and heard the myth, for it apparently arose at a time when the traditional values and cultural forms of the people were being lost and destroyed through contact with an alien European culture of conflicting values. Further, the fact that a chief should choose to leave family and village, for whatever purpose, is itself a violation of an ancient prohibition. The theme is thus timeless and universal, but it is also of special import within a particular historical time and for a specific people.

"He built a house, a small house."

The immediacy of the message of mythological statement has been illustrated through three examples of differing perspectives: the polysynthetic theological implications of the Algonquin myth, which speaks of a continuum of experience of the sacred through the manifest forms and forces of a creation ever creating; the perspective of personal wholeness, thus holiness, through identity with an ideal world of beauty, peace, and harmony of the Navajo myth; and finally the powerful Kathlamet Chinook myth relating to a particular time and cultural

---

[9] I have used the unpublished analysis of this Kathlamet Chinook myth as presented by Dell Hymes in his presidential address to the American Folklore Society in November 1974. This myth was originally narrated to Franz Boas in the 1890s by the Kathlamet elder Charles Cultee.

condition but exposing that universal drama of the human soul—error, punishment-suffering, and final reconciliation. The treatment of these myths, however, remains incomplete without reference to an important dimension of our theme of immediacy: the very medium through which the message is transmitted—the force of oral transmission, what Dennis Tedlock has termed "verbal art."[10]

In addition to the special nature of the Native American languages themselves, as was indicated in the discussion on Navajo chantways, the recounting of the myth is made special through insistence that the telling of the account is serious and potentially dangerous, so that there must be both an appropriate time and place for such telling. Among Native American peoples generally, true myths may be told only after dark and normally in the winter season, after the last thunder of summer and before the first thunder of spring. At this time beings of possible dangerous influence are absent—bears, snakes, and spiders among some peoples. Indeed, severe punishments may occur if this custom is transgressed. The Kiowa believe that if anyone tells a story about their Trickster figure during the day, he will bite their noses off; others believe that one may become a hunchback, or perhaps a snake will come and wrap itself around the teller of the story.

Myths often commence with the phrase, "In the long ago. . . ." This "long ago," it should now be clear, does not refer to a historical period of a linear time past, but usually refers to a qualitative condition of earlier existence which, through the telling of the myth, may be mysteriously reintegrated and realized in the immediacy of the timeless now. Analogous is the "Once upon a time. . . ." of European fairytales, which may be translated as "nowever and forever."

A multitude of rhetorical devices are used by the good teller of stories to convey immediacy. He or she may use the first person, and present rather than past tense, thus telling the account as if really present, even actually engaged in dialogue with the figures of the narrative. As a Zuni once told Tedlock, "You're right with that story, like you were in it." Indeed, I still remember vividly the *Iktomi* (Spider) stories old Black Elk liked to tell; you felt that you were right there with *Iktomi*.

Attention is paid to precise detail, with events in the narrative occurring at specific geographical sites well known in the immediate

---

[10] In clarifying certain contours of this art I drew heavily on two of Tedlock's seminal articles: "Verbal Art" (*Handbook of North American Indians*, vol. 1, chap. 50) and "Towards a Restoration of the Word in the Modern World" (*Alcheringa*, vol. 24, 1976).

environment of the listener. Artful utilization of the human voice conveys the sounds of the animals of the narration, and the lengthening of vowels in adjectives and verbs conveys the sense of duration or distance. The intensity of voice is adjusted to fit the particular action being described, or silence may be used to heighten tension or suspense, or may indicate that the narrator is engaged in personal prayer. Skillful manipulation of language and delivery is utilized to fit the character in question. The rich use of metaphor as well as metonymy—where something is named through its distinctive attribute—serves as a stimulus to the listener's reconstruction of the episode. The beaver, for example, may be referred to among the western Shoshone as "big-tail owner." Ritual enactments often accompany the mythic account, or a multiplicity of props, hand gestures, and mnemonic devices such as the birch-bark scrolls of the Ojibwa. Songs specific to a sacred being of the account may be interjected, or even a personal sacred song of the narrator. There are multiple techniques for bringing the audience into the story, and there are careful means for ending the story to insure the constructive and safe return of the listener from mythic time to the present moment through relating and integrating the one into the other. The use of the concluding "that's why" line again contributes to the impact of experiential immediacy. In versions of the Earth-Diver myth, for example—and to return to where we started—Earth Maker holds the muskrat up by his tail in order to take from his webbed feet that soil of which the earth is made, and in so doing stretches out his tail, just as we find it today.

The endings of Native American accounts, whether of myths or stories, do have moral force, but this is achieved through the use of analogy, or indirectly through the negative activities of the coyote or some trickster figure who engages in all those disreputable things that everyone enjoys hearing of, but always knowing it to be improper conduct. In their great wisdom, Native American accounts, whether of myth or just stories, know where to stop. They never risk alienating their audiences with drawn-out moralizing summaries. In that spirit I shall stretch out no further the muskrat's tail, but shall simply end by saying: "It is so. . . ."

CHAPTER 7

SUN DANCE: SACRIFICE, RENEWAL, IDENTITY

Where a people's vision speaks of life, sacrificial means for recurrent renewal of all life, and suffering for the identity with the source of life—such vision can neither be destroyed, denied, nor ignored.

The annual Sun Dance ceremonies of the Plains Indians of North America give to these peoples—as indeed to all peoples, today as in the past—a message through example affirming the power of suffering in sacrifice, revealing in rich detail the mystery of the sacred in its operations, in all life, and throughout all creation. Where there is no longer affirmation or means for sacrifice, for "making sacred," where the individual loses the sense of Center, the very energy of the world, it is believed, will run out. Such traditions affirm for those who listen, or indeed inevitably for those who do not, that where the sacred in the world and life is held as irrelevant illusion, where evasion of sacrifice in pursuit of some seeming "good life" becomes a goal unto itself, then in the empty and concomitant ugliness of such a life and human-manipulated world, the ordering cycle of sacrifice will and must be accomplished by nature herself so that again there may be renewal in the world.

In accordance with the mood and perspective of this statement, ethnographic description of the particulars of a Lakota, Arapaho, Gros Ventre, Blackfeet, Cree Cheyenne, or Crow/Shoshone Sun Dance is neither appropriate nor necessary. Rather, a composite suggests what is essentially a single language of sacred act and vision, even though expressed by different groups in multiple rich and varied dialects.

Already in the cold darkness of winter's night there are preparations in the Plains for spring's advent and that celebration variously called Dance for World and Life Renewal, Dance Watching the Sun, or the Thirst Dance. Sponsors come forward, advance vows are made by prospective participants, sacred materials are gathered, songs of power are learned and transmitted from the old to the young, and members of these guiding societies meet and prepare for the "moon of grass growing," the time of spring when the power of the sun will return to renew the life of the earth, to bring new strength, goodness, and joy to all of life's beings. It is the one annual occasion when bands or clans, or even several allied nations, may come together to celebrate in solemnity and joy a sacred event, the beginning of a new cycle of life, to insure that the energy of this world and life will be renewed so that the cycle may continue. For three or four days of life-shaping formal rites and ceremonies, and in the additional camp days of preparation and ending, the individual and group will better know the power of suffering in sacrifice.

To construct from timbers brought from the mountains the circular ceremonial lodge, the lodge of "new birth," "new life," the "thirst lodge," is to reenact the creation of world and cosmos. Horizontally, the lodge doorway situated in the east is the place whence flows life in light; from the south comes growth in youth, from the west ripeness, full fruit, and middle age, and from the north completion and old age leading to death, which leads again to new life. At the center of the lodge the most sacred cottonwood tree, rooted in the womb of mother earth and stretching up and out to the heavens, is the axis of the world and the male generative principle. Into and out of this central point and axis of the lodge flow the powers of the six directions. When men in awful ceremony are actually tied to this Tree of Center with the flesh of their bodies, or when women make offerings of pieces of flesh cut from their arms, sacrifice through suffering is accomplished that the world and all beings may live, that life may be renewed, that human beings may realize their identity.

The qualitative powers of the directions and the effective actualization of sacrifice cannot be operative so long as people retain their impurity. Participants initially purify themselves in the little universe of the round sweat lodge, where purifying forces generously released from the rocks of the earth, from air, fire, and water cleanse them and give new life. Indeed, in the days and nights of ritual ceremony to follow means are used to maintain participants in a state of purity through sacrificial concentration on sun or Center, or through the purifying agency of smoke from tobacco, from burning sweet grass and other wild grasses, or sweet sage and cedar.

Special persons are chosen for specific ritual functions, and they become what they personify: Earth Maker, Lodge Maker, and the venerable sacred woman of purity who is Earth herself in all her powers and with all her blessings. Without the presence of this most sacred woman there can be no Sun Dance, for the duality of cosmic forces, the complementarity of male and female, are essential to the creative act and central to the realization of totality. To better translate cosmic realities and processes into immediate visible and effective experience, the bodies of participants are prayerfully painted with earth colors the forms of sun, moon, stars, hail, lightning, and various elements of nature.

At certain times special altars are constructed upon the earth with simple means but of profound import: a place on the earth is cleared and made sacred, directions of the world are delineated always in reference to the Center; humanity's relationship to the cosmos is established, its true "path of life" defined. Ceremonial pipes, themselves portable altars, are ever present with these earth altars. There is an association between the pipe or the straight pipe stem and the central sacred tree, as both are axes, both trace the Way and express the male generative principle, and both speak of sacrifice.

Dancers wear and use whistles made of the wing bone of an eagle to which eagle plumes are attached. In recreating the cry of the eagle in the powerful rhythm of song, dance, and drum, the eagle is present in voice and being; a human being's vital breath is united with the essence of the sun and life. Through such ritual use of sacred form a human becomes an eagle, and the eagle with its plumes is the sun. At each morning's greeting of the new sun, dancers face the east holding their eagle plumes toward the sun's first rays, bathing the plumes in the new light of life, then placing the plumes in movements of purification of the head and of all parts of the upper body, dancing in the meantime to the rhythm of heroic song. Dignified movements of dance facing the sun of the sacred tree are sustained in the suffering of thirst, day and night through the beat of the drum, the heart and life of the world, now one with humankind's own heart and life. It has often been said that the strength of such identity of rhythm is carried within a person's being many months after the celebrations are completed.

Through rich and varied means specific forms of life are celebrated and honored within the lodge. Decorated trees may be planted, pine trees perhaps for the dancer's arbor; moisture-bearing cattails are offered by friends and relatives for the dancer's bed, or chokecherry bushes are planted in conjunction with sacred rites and altars. High in the fork of the sacred tree there is an offering nest for Thunderbird. Some form or aspect of the bison, and an eagle or a rawhide effigy of a human being, is hung upon the tree. Small children sometimes fashion and bring into the lodge pairs of little clay animals: elks, deer, rabbits, kitfoxes, dogs, otters, even grasshoppers. Thus present within the lodge is that which grows from the earth and those who live in the water, who walk on the earth, and who fly in the air. The powers of all things and all beings are present in the holy place.

The Sun Dance is thus not a celebration by humans for humans; it is an honoring of all life and the source of all life that life may continue, that the circle be a cycle, that all the world and humankind may continue on the path of the cycle of giving, receiving, bearing, being born in suffering, growing, becoming, returning to the earth that which has been given, and finally being born again. Only in sacrifice is sacredness accomplished; only in sacrifice is identity found. It is only through suffering in sacrifice that freedom is finally known and laughter in joy returns to the world.

here am I
behold me
I am the sun
behold me
    —Lakota Sun-Rise Greeting Song

CHAPTER 8

THE QUESTION OF "MYSTICISM"

Contemporary uses of the term "mysticism" and its cognates have come to apply them to a wide variety of often disparate phenomena frequently far removed from the early Christian or original Greek senses of the terms. It may indeed be said that mysticism has become so abused, and levels of reality so confused, that in certain contemporary contexts it may actually express the inverse of, or the grossest parody of, those great mysteries and mystics of the great legitimate and orthodox religious traditions of the world.

Examples of abuse and misuse could be cited from a plethora of modern cults, "the new religions," and popular parodies of legitimate spiritual or mystical ways, not to mention experimentations with instant "mystical experiences" afforded through the agencies of various drugs. To underline certain dimensions of such problems one may recall the statement of Aldous Huxley in *The Doors of Perception*, written in 1954:

> It has always seemed to me possible that, through hypnosis, for example, or auto-hypnosis, by means of systematic meditation, or else by taking the appropriate drug, I might so change my ordinary mode of consciousness as to be able to know, from the inside, what the visionary, the medium, even the mystic were talking about.[1]

That contemporary confusions concerning the prerequisite conditions for true spiritual realization abound is eminently comprehensible and evident to many. Under the forces of a pervasive materialistic outlook spreading essentially from the West and causally related to the erosion of the great spiritual legacies, people have become increasingly prisoners of the limits of their vision and the manner in which they experience their world. In seeking release from this constricting experience of a continually changing physical multiplicity, and motivated by a nostalgia for a lost, more-real world of true freedom, many have turned in every possible direction for alternate answers. However, due to the erosion and spiritual impoverishment of one's own

---

[1] Aldous Huxley, *The Doors of Perception* (London: Chatto & Windus, 1954).

proper tradition, or rather, due to our inability in these times to understand the true nature of these traditions, there are left no real criteria
for discrimination, evaluation, and, eventually, choice rooted in true
knowledge. In addition, the quest, often undertaken with the greatest sincerity, may actually be motivated by sentimentality through the
self-will of the ego, or the desire—self-defeating in itself—for some
otherworldly, liberating mystical experience that nevertheless appears
within the realm of limiting phenomena. Under such conditions there
is no guarantee that what is found will not lead to further frustration,
and often—as is the case with altered states of consciousness through
the use of drugs—to sinking within the lower chaotic depth of one's
being, and thus to a deepening intensification of the original problem.

One response to this dilemma, already implied above, may perhaps best be phrased through the following question: Is it still possible, given the force of contemporary circumstances, for a person to
reestablish his or her broken links with one of the great world religious
traditions—that is, with one of those particular and providential expressions of that has been called the *philosophia perennis*, that perennial and timeless wisdom valid "nowever and forever"? That this may
be the only way has been affirmed by an increasing number of scholars
of the sacred, such as Ananda Coomaraswamy, René Guénon, Seyyed
Hossein Nasr, and the great contemporary European theologian and
metaphysician Frithjof Schuon, who has unequivocally stated that

> there is no possible spiritual way outside of the great orthodox tra-
> ditional ways. A meditation or concentration practiced at random
> and outside of tradition will be inoperative, and even dangerous in
> more than one respect; the illusion of progress in the absence of real
> criteria is certainly not the least of these dangers.[2]

It has long been necessary to situate correctly the so-called primitive religions in the context of the world's historical religions, and in
so doing to recognize that in spite of many elements unfamiliar to the
outsider, Native American traditions, at least where there has not been
excessive compromise to the modern world, are in no sense inferior,
but indeed are legitimate expressions of the *philosophia perennis*. The
injustices suffered by these world views, ritual practices, and life-ways,
through ignorance and ill will, through deeply rooted prejudices and
willful falsifications, all commencing with the first European contacts

---

[2] Frithjof Schuon, "Des Stations de la Sagesse," *France-Asie* (Saigon), 1953, no. 85-86,
pp. 507-513 (translation mine).

with the New World, now demand that a reevaluation take place and that proper recognition and respect be given. There are indeed signs today that such positive reassessment is taking place, and what is especially encouraging is the realization on the part of many Native Americans themselves who had lost or neglected their proper religious traditions that such traditions and related life-ways constitute within the world of today not only a viable reality in themselves, but also a valid and powerful response, in terms of fundamental values, to many of the problems faced by the contemporary world. That there is a progressive strengthening of this realization is nothing short of miraculous when one considers the pressures for abandoning these traditions, in the name of "progress" and "civilization," that have been exercised against the people over the past centuries.

One explanation for the current new willingness to understand Native Americans and their life-ways is that, being rooted in this land for thousands of years, the Indians' otherwise very diverse cultures have all come to express rich spiritual relationships with this continent; indeed the forms and symbols bearing these values are all drawn from the details of each people's particular geographic environment. Native Americans lived, and many still do live, what one might call a metaphysic of nature, spelled out by each group in great detail, defining responsibilities and the true nature of that vast web of humankind's cyclical interrelationships with the elements, the earth, and all that lives upon the land. The echoes of this message have caught the attention of at least a few within a society that finally has been forced by hard circumstances to recognize the gravity of the ecological crisis, and thus to seek answers that speak to root causes rather than continually treat the ever-recurring symptoms of the problem.

Many, especially of the younger generations, who formerly had turned to distant lands and seemingly exotic traditions for answers to the problems of the world, have now come to see in expressions of Native American wisdom a meaningful message, because these sacred traditions are rooted in and take their expressions from elements of this very land with which many today, in their alienation, seek meaningful relationships. Further, many individuals discern a deep mystical element in these sacred traditions of the Indian, and it is in something of this vision that they themselves would participate.

However, the problems for the outsider who would personally relate to the sacred vision and practices of the American Indian are just as critical as, or even more problematic than, the attempt to relate to any of the orthodox traditions of East or West. The problem essentially lies in the tendency for the individual not rooted in any tradition to use an alien and thus often exotic religious tradition as a screen upon which to project all that one finds lacking in one's own world. Rarely is the prerequisite effort made to understand the alien tradition on its own terms, through the categories of its proper language, and thus for what it really is in all its profundity and complexity, and with its impelling sacrificial demands. One is too easily satisfied merely to "touch the earth," to nourish one's own personal sentiment and nostalgia, and to hope thereby that somehow a mystic vision of ultimate meaning will automatically and easily come through.

Against the background of the above considerations, it is now possible to ask the following question: If mysticism, in its original and thus deepest sense, is an experiential reality within Native American spiritual traditions, what are the conditions under which such experience becomes operative, and what are some of the contours of its manifestations?

Mysticism, insofar as it is a reality within these native traditions, is not, as the outsider has tended to view it, a vague quality of some supernatural experience that spontaneously comes to individuals whom Providence has allowed to live close to nature. Rather, such mystical experiences are first of all prepared for, and conditioned by, lifelong participation in a particular spoken language that bears sacred power through its vocabulary, structure, and categories of thought, and serves as a vehicle for a large body of orally transmitted traditions, all the themes of which also express elements of the sacred. Secondly, such mystic experiences become more available to those persons who have participated with intensity and sincerity in a large number of exacting rites and ceremonies that have been revealed through time, and that derive ultimately from a transcendent source. There are also, through the nature of the peoples' life-ways rooted in hunting activities, interrelationships informed by the rich oral traditions with all the animal beings and the forms and forces of the natural environment. Further, there is the supporting exposure to a rich heritage of art forms, both visual and audible, many of which are representations of a supernatural experience received by the executor of the form. One may also mention the support offered by the dynamic rhythm of continually living out the myriad details of everyday life, all the forms and acts of which are enriched by the inherent dimensions of the sacred. All these elements and more provide a specific, all-encompassing, supporting frame within which each individual lives out his or her life. Through the conditioning support and force of such spiritual forms and orientations, the individual becomes open to the possibility of receiving in a dream or true vision glimpses of sacred realities borne perhaps by the forms of the natural world, yet more real and permanent than the fleeting relative reality of the immediate world.

Mystical experiences did not come to the people exclusively through the actual vision quest, but also through participation in other rites and ceremonies such as those of purification or the great annual sacrificial Sun Dance, or due simply to the general conditioning powers and sacred content of the totality of their traditions. Good evidence of this is found, for example, in the life of an exceptional man such as Black Elk. His frequent experiences, and the weight of their message and requirements, placed an enormous burden upon him, causing intense suffering throughout his entire life.

Mystical experiences such as the vision, which after all does appear in some phenomenal form, need not be a necessary criterion for, or a proof of, a true and integrated spiritual realization. The experience may simply provide evidence that the recipient has achieved a certain state of realization. Many traditions, it should be recalled, view visions and mystical experiences generally with suspicion, suggesting that they could provide dangerous distractions on the true spiritual way.

What criteria can be used to affirm the spiritual authenticity of religious traditions such as those of the Native Americans, and the reality of mystical experiences to which such traditions give rise?

The tradition in question must have its origins in a sacred source that is transcendent to the limits of the phenomenal world. All the expressions and extensions of this tradition will then bear the imprint of the sacred, manifested in terms appropriate to the time, place, and condition of humankind. The tradition provides the means, essentially through sacred rites, for contact with and ultimately a return to the transcendent Principle, Origin, or by whatever name this is called. True and integrated progress on such an inner journey demands the means for accomplishing the progressive and accumulative integration of the following elements or spiritual dimensions: (1) purification, understood in a total sense, that is, of body, soul, and spirit; (2) spiritual expansion, by which an individual realizes his or her totality and relationship to all that is, and thus integration with, and realization of, the realm of the virtues; (3) identity, or final realization of unity, a state of oneness with the ultimate Principle of all that is. Spiritual expansion is impossible without the prerequisite purification, and ultimate identity is impossible outside the realm of virtue, wholeness, or spiritual expansion.

These themes of purification, expansion, and identity are inherent in all the spiritual ways of the orthodox traditions of the world.

In spite of the initial attractiveness of Indian traditions, because they are rooted in this land and because of their seeming "mystical" qualities they are nevertheless generally inaccessible to the non-Native American. However, by taking the pains to learn what one can from Native American traditions one who as yet is unaffiliated with a true tradition will be aided in knowing what a tradition is in all its complexity, depth, and richness of cultural expressions. It is then possible to undertake the work of rediscovering the roots of what normally, or historically, should be one's own spiritual heritage, and committing oneself to that heritage with the new vision that distance and perspective often allow. This is a way that demands sacrifice, as do all spiritual ways, but it is not an escape, and it has an integrity and a rigor that must always provide hope.

CHAPTER 9

TIME AND PROCESS

Concepts of time and process are central to the nature of the larger realm of a people's world view. To examine these concepts may be one way to address, and hopefully to clarify, certain dimensions of those current and tragic problems of polarizations across and within the world's populations. Examples of accelerating tensions and violence are all too evident in the contemporary proliferation of ideological revolutions and social, economic, and political disruptions, all more or less interrelated with inevitable energy crises as nations vie for control over the world's material resources so that they may continue to build a world of diminishing returns upon the fragile and illusory foundation of the non-renewable.

We are all familiar with those self-serving classification systems by which segments of humanity are identified according to First, Second, and Third Worlds, now extended to Fourth and Fifth Worlds due to the increasing complexities of our current global situation. We are also familiar with associated descriptive terms of less formal language: "developing," "emerging," "backward," or "non-literate," "primitive." It is suspected that our labels and modes of classification do not just describe objective existential situations based on criteria of scientific and technological sophistication, possession and/or access to material natural resources, or quality or type of political system. What is actually projected are idiosyncratic value judgments, not to say latent prejudices, imposed upon world proponents by the First or perhaps Second World populations of such ranking systems.

Imposing value judgments upon others is hardly new to world history; it is indeed most often the material of which history is made. But what is unique today is the scale to which those segments of humanity, whose presiding values are oriented toward unrestrained technological and presiding material advancement, are pressing these values with their concomitant material furniture upon other world populations. The resulting global tensions are multiple, diverse, and complex. But if a comprehensive overview may be risked, there appears to be a polarization between those worlds of scientific/technological sophistication, termed "modern," and those still surviving worlds and mini-worlds whose value orientations may be called "traditional." The former tends to be oriented toward the quantitative, secular materiality of this world, and is essentially sustained by concepts of linear time; the latter inclines toward the qualitative, sacred, otherworldly, and spiritual tendencies and qualities that generally are informed and supported by concepts of cyclical time.

If concepts of time and process are central to particular qualities of peoples' world views, and if such views are instrumental in determining or giving definition to a particular quality of life and culture, then at least some clarification of our personal and global tensions may be furthered through better understanding the nature and implications of these contrasting concepts.

Concepts of time that may be termed linear tend to be of relatively recent origin. It emerged with certain Judaic perspectives, became pervasive in the Western world with the beginnings of the European Renaissance, and was intensified through the rapidly changing ideologies of the Reformation. Obviously a concomitant of the progressive detraditionalization of the Western world, this process has proliferated throughout other once traditional worlds with great rapidity. Our current language forms, in association with and supporting a wide range of patterns of behavior, suggest the degree to which such linear perspectives have come to dominate the structure of our everyday thinking, evaluating, and acting.

In terms of process our time is divided into the categories of past, present, and fixture. Human beings who are oriented toward both past and future are apt to be distracted from the human and spiritual possibilities inherent in the fullness of one's being in the now. Living in the moment of the present allows us to be in immediate and continual interrelationship with the qualities and forces of our natural environment.

Linear time and process is not just a neutral quantitative scale of measurement, but is inseparable from the value orientations that give rise to it in the first place. There is the inevitable assumption that that which came earlier on this scale is somehow inferior to the more recent, or to that in the future toward which we are moving. Idiosyncratic interpretations of Darwinian evolution theories lent support to such assumptions with most gratifying consequences for their adherents, for this new vision sprang from and fed those latent human proclivities, ethno- and egocentricity. Modern people have here found justification for maintaining their assumed inherent, even genetic, superiority over all those other populations of ancient origin who have not yet entered into this new vision of progressive time. Process is now identified with progress, moving onward with ups and downs but inevitably inclining upward.

Such value-laden concepts of time and process completely reversed the traditional cyclical beliefs. They have so permeated our lives and orientations that even certain earlier scholars of the new American anthropological sciences were convinced that the peoples and cultures of their studies, in this case the American Indians, were innately inferior in their humanity and life-ways to people of modern civilization. This belief fed into all those injustices and injuries perpetuated against Native Americans *and* their natural environment, all accomplished under the banner of "manifest destiny," the residues of which still continue to plague us. The Americas have not been the only stages for such tragic play of conflicting values, for such forces have spread to almost all parts of the globe under multiple slogans and justifications through the colonial mentality, through the transference of such a mentality to the new native despots, through prejudices against the grand nomadic traditions. The list goes on.

A core perspective and accompanying human problem, in the concept of linear time and process, is that the line of indefinite extension does not support the situation or experiencing of a center. The linear form suggests, rather, continuity of movement and change from or toward indefinite ends, thus denying the human person the possibility of establishing, of being able to relate to, a true center of permanence that alone can give meaning and direction to change. As has already been mentioned, to forget this truth is to experience a pervasive ever-increasing alienation from nature.

If linear time has thus far been presented as villainous what are the contrasting implications of cyclical time?

With the possible exception of certain Judaic perspectives, the historical religious traditions of the world where they have not been compromised by modernist influences reflect through their rich diversity of means the presiding belief that cyclical, not linear, processes of change are inherent in all of nature in her appearances and modes of operation. Cyclical change, it is further affirmed, can only be possible and meaningful where it proceeds from and is ever in relation to, the unchanging and immutable, by whatever name this be called. It is all too often forgotten that it is not just the historical religious traditions of the world that have guarded this vision, for this is an understanding that is latent, central, and pervasive to probably all of the so-called primitive or tribal peoples of the world. For these are peoples with traditions of generally more ancient origin than the historical religions, and as such they still guard at least vestiges of primordial traditions.

What are some of the messages that come to us from these traditions? Such peoples celebrate the grand mysteries of the cosmos through seasonal, thus cyclical, rites and ceremonies, supported by rich and varied forms of art, architecture, music, and drama. Through such supporting forms and recreating activities change is recognized and honored, but at the same time it is explicitly affirmed that such change is only possible and meaningful in its relationship to the changeless, which is the center of every circle or cycle.

Such a vision of qualitative process in life and thought is always immediately observable and experienced in all the forms, beings, forces, and changes of the surrounding natural world; and at the center of all change, as at the center of all phenomena, there is recognized the indwelling Presence of ultimate Mystery. Where such quality of belief obtains, it inevitably follows that all the forms and beings of nature are held as sacred and thus treated with respect. As a human being, too, at the center partakes of and is surrounded by this Mystery, he or she is not just a part of creation but is one with the totality of all that is. Where this sense for the sacred is lost there is little else that has the necessary force to control our accelerating waste of resources, unless it is the desperate and ultimate threat, the question of our very survival. For it is always nature who will have the last word.

The rhythm of the cycles of the cosmos, the sun and the seasons, recapitulates the cycle of human life as it moves from birth to death. But where this process, inherent in all nature, is understood in traditional cyclical, not linear manner, death inevitably returns to or joins life so that the cycle may continue. The implications of such beliefs to spiritually meaningful eschatologies are of the greatest importance.

They are important also to a host of gerontological problems. Many years ago, living with a very old Lakota Indian in South Dakota, I observed the manner in which he so closely related to little children. There seemed to be no separation. Asked how he understood the child, he replied, "The child is a person who has just come from the Great Mysterious, and I who am an old man am about to return to the Great Mystery. And so in reality we are very close to each other."

Since many primal peoples live nomadic lives based on hunting animals, the cyclical perspective becomes intensified as human activity is integrated into the cyclical movements, migrations, and life cycles of the animals and birds. Humans assume the sacred responsibility for taking the life of living beings, and so become partners, or links, in the cyclical chain of life and death—that there may be life again. It is for these reasons that hunting in such societies is an eminently sacred activity, providing strong means for the human person to identify existentially with the cyclical modes of nature's operation, and thus with that Center which alone makes the process of the cycle possible.

There is another dimension of particular importance to the quality of life, particularly of the nomadic hunters and gatherers who must live in immediate and continuing contact with animals. In his book *Thinking Animals*, Paul Shepard has detailed how contact with animals is "indispensable to our being human in the fullest sense." He says,

> There is a profound, inescapable need for animals that is in all people everywhere, an urgent requirement for which no substitute exists. It is no vague, romantic, or intangible yearning, no simple sop to our loneliness or nostalgia for Paradise. It is as hard and unavoidable as the compounds of our inner chemistry. It is universal but poorly recognized. It is the peculiar way that animals are used in the growth and development of the human person, in those most priceless qualities which we lump together as "mind."[1]

One of our overriding concerns today is to explore means for achieving principles of unity in the current fragmentation of the sciences. Through dialogue between scientists and humanists or religionists, there lies hope that we may relearn what we have forgotten or denied: namely, that change can have neither meaning nor purpose unless it is in relation to the changeless; that the world of phenomenal appearances has neither reality nor message for the realization of the fullness of our humanity unless it is understood in relation to the Absolute.

[1] Paul Shepard, *Thinking Animals* (New York: The Viking Press, 1978), pp. 1-2.

CHAPTER 10

ON BEING HUMAN

One component that is frequently and paradoxically lost sight of is the individual human being; that is, a man or a woman bearing within himself or herself the totality of the richness we usually know best in the outer expressions of those academic disciplines we have come to call by that useful term, the humanities. The ultimate bearer of culture is a person who is religiously human within the context of a traditional heritage.

Many Native American peoples today retain, even though often in fragmented manner, elements of a heritage of ancient primordial origins. Present within all the dimensions, forms, and expressions of this heritage, or rather of these multiple heritages, is a pervasive sense for the sacred. In one manner or another all life is seen to participate in the sacred, all cultural forms express the sacred, so that inevitably within this context the lives of those peoples who live close to their sacred traditions may be called religious, and they are thus beings who are religiously human. Religion pervades all of life and life's activities leading a native person once to remark, "We do not believe our religion, we dance it!"

What then does it mean to be a human person within these Native American cultures? What are the supportive elements, or traditional means of being and seeing, that contribute to this way of being human in a sacred manner?

Webster's Unabridged Dictionary gives this definition for the word *human:* "Man or his attributes, in distinction from the lower animal world; or, relating to man as distinguished from the superhuman, . . . from the divine . . . , belonging to finite intelligence and power."

On both scores these Western definitions are in direct opposition to the Native American sense of being human. For in the Native American worlds, one does not generally find such quasi-absolute dichotomies between humans and what we call animals, nor on the other hand is humankind by definition considered to be absolutely distinct, separated from divine or sacred power or powers. How then do Native American traditions express such an alternate point of view in their beliefs and lives?

In the multiple expressions of Native American lore, in myths and folktales, in rites, ceremonies, art forms, music, and dances, there is the constant implication of, indeed direct references to, the understanding that animal beings are not lower, that is, inferior to humans, but rather, because they were here first in the order of creation, and with the respect always due to age in these cultures, the animal beings are looked to as guides and teachers of human beings—indeed, in a sense their superiors.

According to a Pawnee account, a great council of all the animals (*Nahurac*) meets in perpetual session in a cave under a round mountain (*Pahok*) (actually located, it is believed, near the Missouri River). These animals monitor the affairs of humans wherever they may be on earth, and if a man or a woman is in need or in trouble and seeks aid in humility, perhaps through the vision quest, the council will choose one of its appropriate members—whether winged, four-legged, or crawling—who will then appear to the man or woman and give something of its own power, or present advice that should thereafter guide the person's life.

Beliefs concerning the nature, authority, and meaning of the animals in these traditions may perhaps be summed up in a general manner. In the people's intense and frequent contact with the powers and qualities of the animals including birds and eventually all forms of life, humankind is awakened to, and thus may realize, all that an individual potentially is as a human person. Human completion, wholeness, or religious awakening depends on this receptive opening up to the potentialities and sacred mysteries in the immediate natural environment. Especially in the nomadic hunting cultures, the oneness of essence underlying the visual differences between humans and animals is stressed; on occasion humans and animals may even be interchangeable.

The theme of reciprocal interrelationship between humans and animals, or more generally between humans and all the forms and forces of nature, is translated onto other levels. There appear specific types of theism, for instance, that contrast markedly with certain quasi-absolute Western dichotomies of human/God, nature/supernatural, matter/spirit. One such example is found in the diverse versions of the widespread Algonquin Earth-Diver myth of creation related previously (pp. 64-65). What is often overlooked, however, is that in diving down through the primordial waters for that little bit of earth, the original aquatic beings were cooperating with First Man, Earth Maker, the All-Spirit, or Maheo, who created four things out of the void: water, light, sky-air, and the peoples of the water, but not yet of the earth.

Thus water people were co-participants in the actual creative process itself. This reinforces respect for the aquatic beings, for the earth and humanity's very being is due to their sacrifice. The myth also suggests that the creative principle itself is not locked into some separate time-space orientation; creation is an eternal, ongoing process of the here and now, in which what is created continues to participate. It is eminently important to this perspective that the account has the water beings say of Maheo, "I know," or, "I see, you must be everywhere."[1]

The full import and impact of oral traditions upon those who live by them, whether myth, folktale, song, or everyday language itself, may only be sensed when the meaning and power of words and names in Native American languages is understood. The majority of Native American names, both personal and sacred, refer to animals, or their qualities, and also to other forms of forces of nature. Further, a person's sacred name, which is never used in everyday speech, was normally obtained through prayer and sacrifice in the vision quest. In everyday Native American languages, words and names have sacred power; one uses them carefully for their power affects both speaker and hearer.

In his seminal essay "Verbal Art," Dennis Tedlock reminds us that it is the breath that, universally identified with the essence of life itself, and proceeding from the center of a person's being nearest the heart, bears and fashions the word.[2] Interpersonal verbal communication involves the intermingling of the beings' most sacred element, thus establishing through breath made audible the bond of sacred relationship not only between people, but with all phenomena throughout the cosmos.

Not of the order of the myth perhaps, but still critical in the humanizing of individuals at least on the not-unimportant moral or behavioral level, are those rich traditions of tales involving trickster/hero beings and animals—Coyote, Nanabozo the hare, *Iktomi* the spider. At appropriate times and places the narrator of these tales, through rich and dramatic means, brings to life before the hearer these beings who, in their devious and exciting ventures, define for young and old the perimeters of acceptable behavior. The less-than-human qualities of greed, avarice, selfishness, uncontrolled passions, and sneaky, deceit-

[1] Alice Marriott & Carol K. Rachlin, *American Indian Mythology* (New York: Mentor Books, 1968), p. 39.

[2] Dennis Tedlock, "Verbal Art," chapter 50, *Handbook of North American Indians*, vol. 1, ed. by William C. Sturtevant, Smithsonian Institution.

ful, and unaesthetic behavior are graphically and eloquently spelled out. Children and adults get the point and remember in a manner that lecturing and moralizing never accomplish.

As children grow up within the context of their native traditions they are constantly exposed to forms and actions and ever-widening types of relationships appropriate to the process of becoming a religiously human person. This process commences when the child is in the mother's womb, for especially in this fragile state the being is especially sensitive, it is felt, to all surrounding influences. Barre Toelken tells of a Navajo family close to starvation. The father would not hunt even though there were many deer about, for it was *inappropriate* to take life when a new life was being expected.

The child's first home, the cradle-board of buckskin and specially selected sacred wood (lightning-struck, among the Navajo), provides security and protection for the child not just in its material form but in the sacred powers latent in the wood and the hide, which was once the clothing of the deer itself. A psychological advantage of the cradle-board is that it allows the eyes of the child always to be on the same level as the grown person, the infant never having to look upwards toward an adult. Among the Lakota a young child, especially a girl, is placed in a spider-web type hammock strung out between four trees. In this manner the infant will receive the qualitatively differentiated powers of the four directions of space, and like the spider she may grow up to be an industrious person. Periods of change or crisis in the life of a boy or girl are recognized as sacred moments of transition. Through rites, ceremonies, and initiations (often traumatic as with the Hopi), the child is enabled to enter into adulthood in a manner that integrates or transforms all that the person had been into what he or she now is. In contrast, Western adults have been taught or forced to eliminate from their being the states of the child, so that too often they live only fragments of what they might and should be.

The so-called arts and crafts of a people, found in such imaginative diversity and aesthetic elegance among Native American peoples, are not just utilitarian, as they are usually treated by art historians, but represent external projections of a people's inner vision of reality. (The Museum of Northern Arizona bears above its main portal a statement to this effect: "Herein Are Exhibited Ideas, Not Things.") It is through both creating and living with such ideas, values, sacred powers made tangible, that people are led to realize who they are in their fullest and deepest potentialities, as beings religiously human. So it is with the forms and presences of the sacred *Kachina* beings, whether as so-called dolls, or masked gods, or of the *Yei* who grace the dry-paintings with the healing Power of their presence. To wear the mask is to become that being; to depict the *Yei* is to compel its sacred presence which is transferred to the patient.

Among the peoples of the Plains there is a tradition of two types of paintings on bison hides. One style, painted on the hide of a bison cow and known to art historians as the box and border design, appropriately may be worn only by women, for there is depicted on the hide in highly stylized, abstract manner a kind of vision penetrating into all those inner vital and generative life forces of the cow, manifesting all that is most sacred to womanhood. To wear such a robe is to participate actively in that sacred vision, and thus to be sacred in the fullness of being human as a woman. As a counterpart, the robe worn by a man is made from the hide of a bison bull upon which is painted a dynamic solar device, the sun-burst motif. By wearing such a robe a man participates in the solar power of both the bison bull and the painted sun, reinforcing the essence of all it is to be a man. In the shield paintings of the Plains peoples the protective power is similarly understood to be really present in the depicted form originally received through a vision experience. As with the power that is one with the spoken audible word, so also in the visual and dramatic forms of art; the power of sacredness is really present in the form, whether painted, quilled, sculptured, or danced.

Traditional Native American ways of seeing and living, of being human religiously, have things to tell us about ourselves today. Some of the examples may seem remote from the hard problems of contemporary reality for both Native and non-Native Americans. But I am reminded of a statement written by the late John Collier in 1947 (under the chapter heading "The American Indian and the Long Hope").

> They had and have this power for living which our modern world has lost—as world-view and self-view, as tradition and institution, as practical philosophy dominating their societies and as an art supreme among all the arts.
>
> They had what the world has lost. They have it now. What the world has lost, the world must have again, lest it die. Not many years are left to have or have not, to recapture the lost ingredient.[3]

---

[3] John Collier, *Indians of the Americas* (New York: Mentor Books. 1948), p. 7.

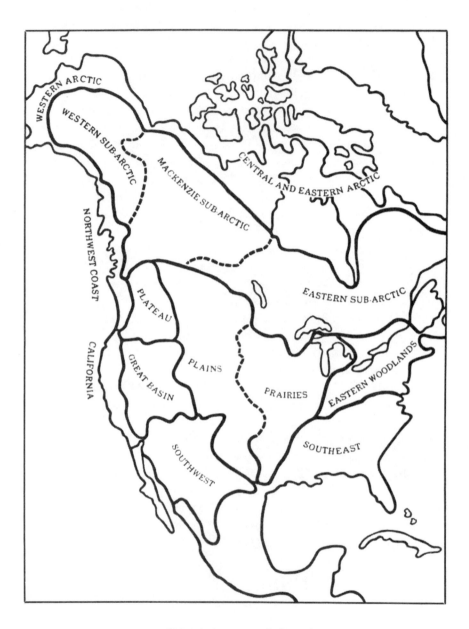

Map of North American Culture Areas

UNPUBLISHED LETTERS OF JOSEPH E. BROWN

After the first visit with Black Elk
September 30, 1947, Manderson, South Dakota
. . . I have been among the Oglala Sioux of Pine Ridge Agency, S.D. for almost three weeks now, and the way has opened in a most gratifying manner. Most of this time has been spent with Black Elk's family in Manderson. Black Elk's son Benjamin has been invaluable as interpreter, and means of contact. As soon as the nature of this visit was understood, I was received most warmly, and every possible assistance was given to me. It was stated that this contact was a "Godsend," and was established just in time—for reasons that I shall explain. . . .

Old Black Elk is 85 and shall not live much longer. He is therefore now anxious to reestablish an Order of the Pipe, and is anxious that I record a history of the Sacred Pipe[1] that he shall dictate as part of this process. Before coming here I had spent much time studying the metaphysics of their Pipe and the accompanying rites, and then realized that in this instrument almost the whole of their ancient doctrine could be preserved. It shall not be difficult for Black Elk to reestablish this order, for in the first place the original Sacred Pipe is still preserved by a holy man—Elk Head, who lives at Cherry Creek, in the Cheyenne Agency, S.D. (These people are also Oglala, and speak Lakota.) Also in talking with several of the old men here I have found that almost all still keep their pipes, and have never lost their respect for this sacred object. Much of their understanding of it has however, been lost, but it would not be difficult to reestablish this, for they possess all the requirements, and are especially humble and sincere, having a most wonderful disregard for the things of this world. . . .

When leaving Black Elk, I was presented a sacred red-stone pipe, and a bag of sacred tobacco. This pipe was made long ago by a holy man, Little Deer, and the possession of it I am told shall open the way for me among not only the Sioux but also among the other Plains nations. I mention this only that you may know how well I

---

[1] Brown's reference here is to the original Sacred Pipe brought to the Sioux people by the White Buffalo Calf Woman. The Sioux people and many other tribes often use the words "sacred pipe" when referring to all pipes. "Sacred Pipe" and "Pipe" is capitalized when it refers to the original Sacred Pipe of the Sioux people, but it is not capitalized when it refers to any other pipe or all pipes of the Sioux people.

was received, and that the sacred hoop of these people has not been broken. . . .

After a visit with the Blackfeet

October 28, 1947

After being with the Blackfeet I understood that one must not be too hasty in judging the disintegrating influence of the tourist. In the summer many take their lodges and go into the mountains of the Park, and sing, dance, and take money for permitting the tourists to take their picture. But several old people told me that although they earn money from the tourists by doing this, at the same time they are being paid for living the way they wish to live, in the open, and in a ○; and when they put on their dances, the old people are conscious of the meaning. In other words, they tolerate the tourists and take what they can from them.

Most of my time here was spent with an old man, a chief, by the name of "Crow Chief" Reevis. He lived far away from town, on a handsome river, with magnificent mountains in the background—and there through many evenings we had long talks. He speaks English when discussing ordinary affairs, but in discussing spiritual beliefs, he always uses his own tongue. His daughter-in-law was an excellent interpreter for me. Crow Chief is a splendid man, and was lodge maker for the Sun Dance last summer, and is one of the most handsome men I have ever seen. He was most interested in my reason for being there, and was fully conscious of the crisis of the present time, and said he was trying to impress this on the young people. Crow Chief told me of a group among them who meet every Saturday night and prayed until the morning. The pipe is the ritual object used mostly by them, and their songs are of the greatest excellence.

After a visit with the Crow

October 28, 1947

The Crow are very strong in their old ways, and the people generally take their own religion very seriously. This is even reflected in their outer appearance. They are all extremely friendly and anxious to talk of anything. Until several years ago, the agent of this Reservation was Robert Yellowtail, a Crow.[2] He was very well-educated, but preferred the old ways. During the day, he would work in the office, but in the

[2] Robert Yellowtail was the first American Indian superintendent of a reservation. Yellowtail Dam and Yellowtail reservoir in south-central Montana are named after him.

evening he would live in his tent, wear traditional clothes, and would sing while beating on his drum. His choice and example was undoubtedly a great stimulus to his people, even though almost all his efforts were political; he often goes to Washington, and is there now, and so I was unable to talk with him. His family was most pleasant to me, in part because his wife is the cousin of a Sioux friend of mine.

A key man among the Crow is Barney Old Coyote. He was the lodge maker last summer, and explained to me with perfect clarity the metaphysics of the Sun Dance and the pipe. He explained how the Sun Dance Lodge represents the Universe, the tree of life at the Center, being the axis, and its branches extending up above and out of the Universe into the Infinite. There are three rings painted on the Pole, representing, he explained, the three worlds: body, soul, and Spirit. The axis is everywhere, and is of course within every being, and the ultimate purpose of the dance, after purification and sacrifice, is for the participant to move from the periphery to the Center, with which he ultimately identifies himself. In the same way he explained the pipe. And in the same manner Old Coyote explained to me about the Beaver Lodge, an initiatory organization possessed by the Crow and Blackfeet. Upon initiation, they are taught certain songs that are repeated all the time to be used as a type of *mantra*. Although their terminology is different from other religions, when I explained to him that the repetition of a prayer of the heart can establish an identity between the sincere spiritual seeker and the Creator (as well as one can explain that which cannot be explained), he immediately said that that was also the ultimate end of their organization. This is of course a very ancient organization, and one wonders how long it has remained dormant, as initiatory organizations often do when they lack a saint. However, it is still there potentially; they meet every week, and I met several who know the songs. . . .

I was prayed over by Old Coyote and his wife, and might mention what this involves. The sacred bundle used was made by John Trehero,[3] a Shoshone. The bundle was opened, and the contents spread out on the table. One cannot enumerate all the things—weasel pelts, little medicine bags, feathers of all sorts, some painted this way:

---

[3] Dr. Brown is referring to John Trehero, the Shoshone Sun Dance chief who introduced the Shoshone Sun Dance to the Crow tribe in 1941. Trehero died in 1985 at the age of 102.

and cedar twigs, bags of paints, etc. First, cedar is burned on a coal, and all the objects are purified in the smoke. Then red circles were painted around each wrist, representing the halos around the Sun and Moon (pairs are of course holy, especially the hands which do His work). Then, as an eagle bone whistle is blown (the breath of life, as he explained), the seven eagle feathers are fluttered all over the person and are continually purified in the smoke. The smoke is also blown all over the person. Then the feathers are held very tightly against the chest, and with the hand remaining against the chest, the feathers are swiftly pulled away—wrung out so to speak, so that the Power from the feathers is transformed to you; for as he explained, the eagle represents the Great Spirit, and thus the feathers represent His actual Presence. After this, I was asked to say a prayer, . . . and then I was given a "medicine" made from sacred herbs (this was just like the Christian Communion, they explained). (Old Black Elk explained to me that some of the "medicines" of the holy men are made from 550 different herbs, as well as parts of the bear being mixed in; they are thus very *wakan*, holy.) . . .

With Black Elk in Colorado
October 28, 1947
It is good to be back with Black Elk; we are now in Julesburg, Colorado. . . . The headdress of many feathers is not worn by the Sioux women, but they do wear a single fluffy feather from the breast of the eagle (who represents the Great Spirit in their hair). The feather stands for the Presence of *Wakan-Tanka*, Black Elk explained. Incidentally, at death a man's headdress and a woman's feather is kept by the family along with the scalp lock from the center of the top of the head. The two are kept together for a year, in order to protect the *Orenda*.[4] It is often taken outside by the family, and often the headdress is hung on a pole beside the tipi, and is of course considered very *wakan*. At the end of a year, both are buried. . . .

Last week I took Black Elk to Denver in my truck and we spent several hours looking for a place to sleep. Most of the hotels would not take in Indians and I was very discouraged. It was getting dark and late, and we were tired. We finally found a room in a run-down area of Denver. The place was very dilapidated. When we entered the room, Black Elk announced that he sure felt dirty here in this city

---

[4] *Orenda* is an Algonquin term meaning the spiritual aura or the potentiality of the departed spirit.

and that we must have a sweat to cleanse ourselves. He proceeded to make a Sweat Lodge right there in the middle of the shabby room. He reached under the back of the brick chimney and found some loose bricks. He heated them up in a pan of coals, and we had our sweat ceremony under the table with a blanket over it. We felt better after our purification. . . .

In Black Elk's home
November 19, 1947, Manderson, South Dakota
. . . We are now back in Manderson and have started on our real work; it is progressing slowly, for there are many interruptions; but I am tremendously encouraged, as you shall understand from the following. . . .

Every few days we take a trip to one of the small settlements about here, and contact the leading holy men, to whom Black Elk explains his plans, why I am here and has me talk to them a bit. Everywhere there has been great enthusiasm and all have promised him their support, for, as you know Black Elk is regarded as their spiritual leader here on the Pine Ridge Reservation; he is also perhaps the oldest of all. It has been a great thing for me to meet these men, precisely the ones we are looking for; probably I could find them no other way. In Pine Ridge we have contacted Spotted Crow—a splendid old man—Stabber, and Red Cloud (son of the old chief); here at Manderson, Kicking Bear (son of the High Priest) and others; at Kyle, American Horse (son of the great chief) and Little Warrior.

I cannot praise Little Warrior highly enough; he is as integrated and concentrated a person as I have yet met, quite on a par with Black Elk, and appropriately enough he is the one Black Elk has chosen to succeed him as leader of the religion of the Pipe. He is about seventy-six, but virile and energetic, and his energies are devoted towards following in his ancient religion. You can thus understand how warmly we were received. . . . Little Warrior is strong on the Ghost Dance, and participated much in this in his youth. His wife's father, Bites the Eagle, was one of those who went to visit *Wovoka*,[5] and so Little Warrior has much of the original sacred material for this dance. He told me that if they could get the assurance of the government not to interfere, he and many followers would be dancing within a few weeks. He said that there are any number still living who remember

---

[5] *Wovoka* is the Piute prophet who was the recipient of the first dream vision of the Ghost Dance. People from many tribes sent people to visit *Wovoka* in order to adopt the Ghost Dance for their own tribal use. Black Elk describes the phenomenon of the Ghost Dance in detail in *Black Elk Speaks*.

this dance, and would be eager to participate once again. He told me that ultimately the only purpose of this dance was to see or be at one with *Wakan-Tanka*. . . . In any case, Little Warrior said, should this be impossible, they still have the religion of the Pipe, and this the government cannot interfere with; it also contains all the essentials of their whole religion.

These men, and several more, shall constitute, I believe, the intellectual and spiritual center that we had hoped for. In about three weeks or a month they are all coming to Manderson, and with many ceremonies, the Order of the Pipe shall be established. Names shall also at this time be given to Father Gall[6] and myself. Father Gall's name shall be *Lakota Ishnala*, Lone Sioux, and mine *Channumpa Yuhan Mani*, He Walks with the Sacred Pipe. Also starting tomorrow, we shall begin the work of recording the history of the Sacred Pipe, for Black Elk is the only one who knows it completely. This shall, we hope, be published, so that the followers of this tradition shall have access. Publishing it should not be difficult, since it is unique material. . . .

It is often difficult for those who look on the tradition of the American Indians from the outside, or through the "educated" mind, to understand their preoccupation with the animals, and with all things in the Universe, as is shown in their myths and hundreds of songs. But for these people, as of course for all traditional peoples, every created object is important simply because they know the metaphysical correspondence between this world and the real World. No object is for them what it appears to be, but is simply the pale shadow of a Reality, and the instructed American Indian understands these correspondences, both horizontal (with the curing rites, etc.) and vertical. Furthermore, they possess a very real hierarchy, and it is for this reason that every created object is *wakan*, holy, or has a power, according to the level of the spiritual reality that it reflects. Thus many objects possess power for evil as well as for good and every object is treated with respect, for the particular "power" that it possesses can be transferred into you. Of course, they know that everything in the Universe has its counterpart in the soul of man. Thus Black Elk says that the Spotted Eagle is really within us. The Indian humbles himself before the whole

---

[6] Father Gall was a Trappist monk at the Abbaye Notre Dame de Scourmont in Belgium and a close friend of Dr. Brown, who acted as an intermediary in correspondence between Father Gall and Black Elk. Even though most of the references to Father Gall have been deleted from this collection of letters, the remaining references provide an insight into Black Elk's relationship with the Catholic Church. See also a letter to Father Gall dated December 26, 1947, p. 113.

of creation (especially when "lamenting") because all things were created by *Wakan-Tanka* before him, and deserve respect, as they are older than man. However, although the last of created things, man is also first and unique, since he may know *Wakan-Tanka*.

An important aspect of the pipe is the following: the sacred tobacco, or *kinnik-kinnik*, that is burned in the bowl, represents the Universe and also man. He who fills the pipe with the sacred tobacco represents the Creator in the act of creation. In smoking the pipe, the Universe, including man—or ignorance—is consumed in the fire, which is *Wakan-Tanka*; and thus a cycle is completed. *Wakan-Tanka* is thus represented under the aspects of Creator and Destroyer. The progression from the mouthpiece, through the stem (the Islamic *Siratu'l Mustaqim*[7] or the Hindu *Deva Yana*[8]) to the Center, and then the liberation, you of course know of.

Black Elk has taken a great interest in his son, Father Gall; he talks of him often, and is having several things of buckskin made for him. He is also sending him his necklace made of sacred deer hoofs, and we are sending him a pipe and sacred tobacco. It of course means much to Black Elk to have the support of a Christian Father, for the priests here have been continually after Black Elk to give up his "heathen practices," and "works of the devil," and to participate fully and only in Catholicism. *Black Elk Speaks* did not acknowledge (much to the anger of the Church) that Black Elk was baptized some forty years ago, and was responsible for the "conversion" of many Indians. Black Elk says that he is sorry that his present action towards reviving Lakota spiritual traditions shall anger the priests, but that their anger is proof of their ignorance; and in any case *Wakan-Tanka* is happy; for he knows that it is His Will that Black Elk does this work.

In Black Elk's home
November 27, 1947, Manderson, South Dakota
Black Elk was most pleased to know the dream of the flower, and wishes to tell this woman, that as her sick flower grew and bloomed, so he believes that the once dying tree of his nation shall now also grow and bear fruit; and his people, or at least some of them, shall again be walking the Red Road. He has told me (as we know) we have reached the end of a cycle; and leading into the beginning of the next new cycle there is a very narrow bridge. It is his hope that a few of

[7] Literally "the straight path."

[8] Literally "the Way of the Gods."

his people—together with the holy men of other nations—shall walk across this narrow way.

I do not know whether you have known it—I had not until recently—that the Indian holy men possess quite completely a knowledge of the "Eye of the Heart" (*Chante Ishta*). I shall quote several statements Black Elk has made on this.

> I am blind and do not see the things of this world; but when the Light comes from Above, it enlightens my Heart and I can see, for the Eye of my Heart sees everything; and through this vision I can help my people. The heart is a sanctuary at the Center of which there is a little space, wherein *Wakan-Tanka* dwells, and this is the Eye. This is the Eye of *Wakan-Tanka* by which He sees all things, and through which we see Him. If the heart is not pure, *Wakan-Tanka* cannot be seen, and if you should die in this ignorance, your soul shall not return immediately to *Wakan-Tanka*, but it must be purified by wandering about in the world. In order to know the Center of the Heart in which is the Mind of *Wakan-Tanka*, you must be pure and good, and live in the manner that *Wakan-Tanka* has taught us. The man who is thus pure contains the Universe within the Pocket of his Heart (*Chante oqnaka*).

In referring to *Wakan-Tanka*, the Sioux make a distinction between *Tunkashila* and *Ate*, "Grandfather" and "Father" (Godhead and God). "Grandfather" refers to *Wakan-Tanka* before and beyond all creation: Infinite and Unqualified. "Father" refers to *Wakan-Tanka* as Creator, Sustainer, or Destroyer, God in act, Qualified. In the same way they make the distinction, in referring to Mother Earth, between *Ina*, "Mother," and *Unchi*, "Grandmother." "Grandmother" is the ground or substance of all things, while "Mother" refers to Her creation, or to Her in the act of producing in conjunction with *Ate*.

According to Black Elk, the Sioux divide a total cycle into four periods of life symbolized by the four eagle feathers on the sacred hoop, used in the Sun Dance and otherwise. The first age is the Stone, the second the Bow, the third the Fire, the fourth the Pipe. There are also four stages through which every created thing passes; these are represented by the four Directions and the four Winds. The first is South, which is yellow, and which is the Source of life and also the End, and this is the first age in a historical period. The second is West, which is black; the third is North which is white; and the fourth is East which is red. Black Elk of course says that we are now in the fourth stage, and that a great disaster is impending which shall bring this cycle to a close.

In Black Elk's home
December 14, 1947, Manderson, South Dakota

You once asked about Elk Head, former keeper of the Sacred Pipe. It seems that he certainly was a qualified person—indeed it was from him that Black Elk received the sacred history, which we are now recording. When Elk Head gave this history to Black Elk, he said that he must do so, for he knows that so long as this history is handed down and known by the people, they shall have a center and shall live. But their people shall come to an end when this history is no longer known. I might also mention here that the rest of the ancient history, which Black Elk knows, was received from Breast—famed Sioux historian.

Elk Head had two sons, but both were unqualified to be keepers of the Pipe. The Pipe was thus handed down to Elk Head's daughter [Martha], who married a certain Bad Warrior.[9] The Pipe then went to Eli Bad Warrior, who had little or no traditional instruction. He does, however, fear the power of the Pipe, and this is good, for it shall keep it from being profaned. I have also recently been told that Bad Warrior is willing to give up the Pipe should the people wish it, and so it seems quite certain that this shall happen in the spring, and Black Elk shall help choose a qualified person.[10]

I was told that during the time when Elk Head's daughter was the keeper of the original Pipe bundle, two men made careful drawings of the Sacred Pipe and took these to Rapid City, where they made much money showing these to curious tourists. On their way home they were both struck by lightning and they and their pictures were destroyed! I also have been told that some years ago the agent here sent two policemen to confiscate the Pipe, and bring it to him—I believe he intended to give it to a museum. The Pipe was brought to the agent's office, but all that night the agent could not sleep because of the constant bellowing of a buffalo calf in the room where the Pipe was kept. In the morning he had the policemen return the Pipe. Later

---

[9] Elk Head's daughter's married name was Martha Bad Warrior.

[10] Martha Bad Warrior passed the original Sacred Pipe to her son, Eli Bad Warrior. Some years after the date of this letter, Eli Bad Warrior passed the Pipe on to his sister, Lucy Bad Warrior. In 1966 Lucy was told in a dream to pass the Pipe to her grandson, Arvol Looking Horse, who was only 12 years old at the time he became the keeper of the Pipe bundle. Arvol Looking Horse is still the keeper of the Pipe bundle and lives near Green Grass on the Cheyenne River Sioux Reservation.

that year one of the policemen was struck by lightning and was killed; and the other soon died of some disease. . . .[11]

Tomorrow I travel to the four quarters and gather up our key leaders: Little Warrior, Good Lance, Red Cloud, and Spotted Tail. They shall remain here for three days, during which time our plans shall be laid, and our course of action decided upon. It shall be a great thing to see these venerable old people together again. Young Black Elk has just shot two bucks to feed them with, and I expect there shall be much singing and dancing. Names shall also be given to Father Gall and myself. Then on the 18th, all day, a great pipe ceremonial shall be held here in Manderson. Black Elk shall lead it, Little Warrior helping, for there shall probably be over a hundred old people; they are coming from all over the reservation. After this I shall feel that "my" work here has been finished (except for the recording, which may take some time) for I know that these people shall carry on themselves. But the four elders mentioned above, and of course Black Elk, have told me that they hope I shall keep in touch with them after I leave. . . .

In Black Elk's home (after a *Yuwipi* ceremony with Little Warrior)
December 26, 1947, Manderson, South Dakota
. . . The majority of the Indians shall always be poor, for as soon as they get something it is given away. Their generosity has certain spiritual compensations, for it keeps them in the lap of Nature from which they gain much inner strength; for in this period Nature remains in her original purity, uncontaminated by the darkness of men's souls. Indeed many Indians have expressed to me their gratitude to *Wakan-Tanka* for allowing them this privilege.

Crazy Horse and Sitting Bull were among the few chiefs who never compromised with the white man. No man is held in more veneration here than Crazy Horse—he is always being talked about when any group gathers. His place of burial is still a mystery, and probably always shall be, which is good; but it is believed that he is not over a mile from here.

Little Warrior (*Ozuyé Jikala*) and his wife, daughter of "Yellow Breast" (a nickname—Black Elk does not remember his true name) who visited *Wovoka* and brought the Ghost Dance to the Sioux, spent this past week with us. There were ceremonials day and night, and singing and talks concerning the revival of the religion of the Pipe.

---

[11] Both of these stories were confirmed in recent conversations with Arvol Looking Horse, the current 19th generation keeper of the original Sacred Pipe.

In the evenings up to fifteen people would gather and Little Warrior would officiate at the pipe ritual, which as you may know takes on many varied forms, according to the vision of the one who conducts it. In the essentials, all ways are the same.

All sit in a great circle, with Little Warrior in the center (a magnificent looking person: tall, long hair, penetrating eyes, kindly, a marvelous humility and tremendous energy for seventy-six years of age). A strand of incense (sweet grass) is lit from a coal and this he passes around the circle sun-wise, so that each person may purify their hands, face, hair, arms, and body. Earth is brought from the outside and is put in the center, on which a coal is placed, and sweet grass burned here from time to time. He places four flags around him on each quarter, Yellow for the South, Black for the West, White for North, and Red for East. The altar in the center is now constructed of tobacco—a pinch on the South, then one on the West, North, East, thus forming a square; then these four quarters are joined by a circular line of tobacco: a pinch is placed in the center (*Wakan-Tanka*) and then some is sprinkled all about inside. All this is done with appropriate songs of the most marvelous quality, and several drums are used.

His two pipes are then laid alongside the altar stems to the West. His "medicine" equipment is laid about the altar—one made from the sac of a young buffalo bull, one from a deer's hoof, a piece of buffalo hide, eagle bone whistle, tail of the black deer, etc., all representing the Universe. A string of little sacs of tobacco, joined with one string (similar to a Christian or Muslim rosary) is laid around the altar, representing the camp circle and hoop of the nation. The offerings of those who wish to ask questions during the ceremony are laid together on the North of the altar. Beside the altar a tall cherry stick with fruit on it is placed upright, and at the top an eagle feather is tied (Tree of Life and Great Spirit).

Now everything is purified with sweet grass smoke, and the pipes especially are made sacred. The pipes are now filled, and this is the most impressive part of the ceremony, for the four Quarters and everything in the Universe, is gathered into one point, the bowl of the pipe where the sacrifice is to take place. During the filling of the pipes, the Pipe Song is sung, which tells in six verses the history of the Pipe. This holy song is the most powerful of any song I have ever heard, and with the two drums, and all singing in very loud voices, the "aesthetic shock," if one may call it that, is tremendous. When *Wakan-Tanka* is mentioned all raise their hands, and then touch earth. I believe this song shall do much in furthering our work, for we sing it all the time now, and it is spreading all over; I even find many of the young people around here singing it as they ride along in the evening.

To fill the pipes, a handful of tobacco is taken and blessed. A pinch is held to the West, and is drawn along the stem to the bowl, where a circular movement is made before filling. Likewise a pinch for the other Quarters, North, East, South, Heaven, Earth, and then the bowl is filled up. At the beginning of one of these ceremonies, Little Warrior gave me one of his pipes, which I was to hold in front of me, stem up. (He had told me before that he was giving it to me, and wished me always to keep it, for it was the first pipe that he had made himself, and had used it many times in lamenting; a splendid gift which bears many blessings and much spiritual strength).

There now comes a part of the ceremony, which is difficult to explain, for it is less purely metaphysical and belongs to a more inter-mediary realm. For my part it is perfectly valid so long as a qualified person carries it on, and so long as it is kept in its proper place, and is known for what it is. You may not know much about the *Yuwipi*, and so I had best explain a bit. Perhaps it can best be called "ceremonial magic." To practice *Yuwipi* one has to be given special powers by the spirits, and these "spirits" answer questions for the person, and find lost objects and cure the sick. This gift was given to Little Warrior by the Owl, and he is certainly a person qualified to use it. But although Little Warrior was chosen to know the things of this realm, he is also a metaphysician and sage of the first order—a true holy man in every part.

For the *Yuwipi* ceremony the room is made completely dark. The pipe is still in the center at its alter and a most wonderful singing and drumming begins. Little Warrior sings the songs. Soon the rattles start to shake and fly about the room at an incredible rate, sending out sparks when they hit—the drum too starts to fly about the room. There is silence off and on when questions are asked—usually of doctrinal nature—except when the one making the offering wishes to find something (I have seen Little Warrior or his spirits find things in a most miraculous way), and the spirits too, ask you questions which keep you on your toes.

When it is all over, the room is illuminated and the pipes are lit and offered to the directions: Heaven, Earth, West, North, East, and South and are sent sun-wise around the circle to be smoked. They are then emptied and blessed by rubbing sage over them. It was at this point Little Warrior's pipe and bag were given to me, with a prayer. Little Warrior then took this pipe back, and passing it sun-wise let each person draw his hand along the stem, as a final parting to the pipe, which was leaving the people. It was than handed back to me.

I should mention that a small part of every food to be used in the feast had been placed in a bowl in the center. This was now blessed, and the women now brought in great quantities of venison, soup, herbs, *wasna* (a bread), *wojapi*, made from buffalo berries, and many other Lakota dishes—all very excellent. All this usually lasts until about 3:00 a.m.

There are two things Little Warrior is particular about. He will never conduct a ceremonial unless all are seated on the floor, with shoes off. He also likes to have each participant hold a sprig of sage.

The ceremonials, all different, but all centering around the pipe, went on every night for about five days. Then on the 18th we had the large pipe ceremonial at Manderson. I had sent out notices to all the old Lakota whom we wanted to contact, and perhaps about a hundred came with their teams from all over. . . . This was of course the great day for Black Elk, for his vision was now being realized, and he was as happy and excited as a child. He and Little Warrior painted their faces red, and put on their best clothes, and what traditional clothing they had. Little Warrior wore a handsome black blanket, with beaded circles in white and red on the sides and back, and ribbons for the four Quarters hanging from the center of each beaded circle. Never have I seen a priest officiate at a rite with more dignity, confidence, and majesty.

All—men, women, and children—sat in a large circle, perhaps 50 yards across and the food for the feast was placed in the center. Earth with coals was also placed in the center from which the sweet grass was lighted, and all the people purified themselves. Little Warrior constructed the tobacco altar, and Black Elk with dignity and tears said a long prayer. . . . The two pipes were laid on the ground with stems facing West (he used the one given to me), which, with the sacred song, were filled. Black Elk again gave a long prayer, and then Little Warrior held aloft two eagle feathers which he fluttered above and to the four Quarters, doing this slowly and with great majesty—looking much like the eagle himself—with his long arms. The pipes were then lit and passed around sun-wise, one starting from the East and one from the West. Each participant, even the children, took a puff, and as Little Warrior went around with the pipe, he looked precisely as a priest giving the Holy Communion, which it, of course, is. He then returned the pipe to me and said that now wherever I go I should take his people with me, for they are within this pipe. Many of the old men, still strong and handsome, now arose and one by one gave a short speech, most of them expressing that they had neglected the pipe given to them by *Wakan-Tanka*, and that it is now a necessity that they use it once again. One said that the civilization of the white men is near to destruction; but it is his hope that a few of his people shall construct a bridge, leading from the end of this period into the next, and this shall be done with the help of the pipe.

The next day when I took Little Warrior and his wife home (a six-hour drive), they both sang holy songs and prayed all the way. She too is a very holy person. Little Warrior is, I believe, as holy as Black Elk. He always remained true to his own way, and has retained his original purity, so to speak. . . . When he enters a house he burns sweet grass and purifies himself. It is good to watch him combing his long hair in the morning. He burns sweet grass, holds his comb in it, offers it up, and then takes a few strokes. The same is then done for the four Quarters. I explained to Little Warrior about the prayer of the heart, and he said they use the same thing. The most common being the repetition of *Tunkashila Wakan-Tanka*, or just *Tunkashila;* or: "*Wakan-Tanka* have pity on me!" Even now, he said, I have been doing this. (Little Warrior and his wife now lead the annual Sun Dance held in July, and have done so since Black Elk has been unable because his eyesight continued to deteriorate to the point he was virtually blind.)

Black Elk too prays all the time, and perhaps he has gone beyond the need of the external rite? I might mention that Little Warrior always places himself below Black Elk, who is the elder and thus the superior. But Black Elk is so old that he is helpless without assistance, and this is why up to now, without support, he had done nothing about the pipe. It is good to know that after his death, these people shall have in Little Warrior a spiritual leader who has tremendous energy, and who shall do much towards regaining the lost ground.

I believe that I shall not leave for the Hopis until the end of January, for this work is going very slowly indeed. . . . We have, however, finished the history of the bringing of the Sacred Pipe, its use in the "Keeping of the Spirit," the *Inipi* (literally "live again") Sweat Lodge and are now working on the most interesting part of all: the lamenting. Black Elk mentions that this is really similar to the Sun Dance, except it is an individual thing, and is participated in by all the people all the time.

On a remote mountaintop, a sacred place is made with four poles for the four directions, and one for the Center. The only movement the one lamenting can make is from the Center to West, to Center, and so on: Center to North and back to Center, etc. You cannot go around, but must always go from the Center to the periphery and then return. You can sleep wherever you wish, and a sacred bed of sage is made for this.

In Black Elk's home
December 26, 1947, Manderson, South Dakota
Extract of a separate letter written on this same date to Father Gall.

All day this last Sunday, your father prayed for you,[12] and had us do so too when we went to church. You were remembered in our grace for Sunday dinner, and all evening he talked of you. Almost miraculously on Monday your letter arrived, and I wish I could convey to you the great joy which it brought to Black Elk. On Christmas Eve we all (except for Black Elk for he was tired) went to midnight Mass. When we returned on Christmas morning your father was sitting up in bed, and seemed extremely happy over something—he told us that he had visited *Lakota Ishnala* in Belgium, had had a good talk with him, and had just now returned. He said that he had told you that you shall always really be a Lakota, for when you die your body, which is of earth, shall remain with the white men, but your soul shall return to us. He also said that he now sees that he perhaps should have given you a better name: Two Men, for in appearance you are a white man, but in reality you are an Indian.

Later Note by the author: On this day and time that there was a terrific thunderstorm around the tower where Father Gall lives. It was strange to have a thunderstorm at that time of year. Father Gall has not said what message he received from Black Elk in the storm, only that he took hold of his sacred pipe and he prayed.

In Black Elk's home
January 8, 1948, Manderson, South Dakota
Most of the Sioux I've met are completely disinterested in any question of their origin. They possess a marvelous freedom from the limiting conditions or consideration of time and place and many continually remind me of what must have been the condition of the soul of primordial man. When questioned on their origin they usu-

---

[12] Black Elk officially adopted Father Gall as his son. (Footnote 6 provides additional information about Father Gall.)

ally reply that they have come from *Wakan-Tanka* or from *Unchi* (Grandmother), and to Her they shall return. "*Wakan-Tanka*," they say, "placed us specially on this great island. . . ."

It is interesting that the Sioux I've spoken with believe that long ago all the people of North America were one and spoke a common Siouan language. During that time they all lived in peace, but later dispersed in three directions: West, North, and East, but not South for that is the abode of Life and Death, and only birds and spirits go and come from there. Each of the new nations developed a different language, but the Sioux retained the original.

Symbolism of the "four directions"

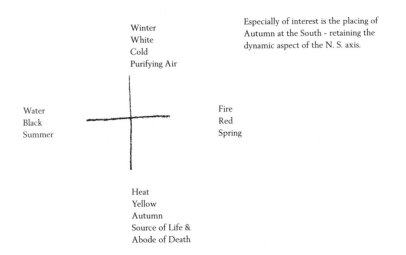

Winter
White
Cold
Purifying Air

Especially of interest is the placing of Autumn at the South - retaining the dynamic aspect of the N. S. axis.

Water
Black
Summer

Fire
Red
Spring

Heat
Yellow
Autumn
Source of Life &
Abode of Death

When the world ends the Lakota believe that the South star shall meet the North or Pole star, and there will be many falling stars, and they will burn up the earth. The winds shall blow from the East rather than from the West (the reverse of the Poles). The Sun will turn red, and the moon will turn blue. These are the red and blue days, so often referred to, but which have rarely been understood by scholars. Black Elk agrees that the presence of these two "days" may be understood in three ways: the death of the self or ignorance here and now; the apparent death of the physical being; or the end of a world, or total cycle. Not very long ago, all the Sioux participating in their traditions wore a blue spot on the forehead—so they would be known by the old woman who stands where the Milky Way divides in the southern heaven. She is appropriately named *Mava Owi Cha Paha*, She Who

Pushes Them Over the Bank. At the end of the world the good go to the right, and the bad she pushes to the left.

In Black Elk's home
January 24, 1948, Manderson, South Dakota
. . . Worthy to mention is a young Lakota here by the name of Theodore Means (He Holds the Lance). His grandfather was Fast Thunder, holy man and chief. Theodore, his wife, and his aged and most charming mother have been very kind to me here, and he has shown much interest in what we are doing. He was in the war and under fire a good deal; at that time he understood the falsity of the white man's civilization and saw what it was leading to. He then vowed that if he should return, he would go back to his old way of life. This he has done to a certain extent, having lamented twice with his pipe. He wishes to participate more fully in his tradition. . . . He went to the Catholic Mission School in Pine Ridge, up to about tenth grade, but was told to leave when he disagreed with the priests concerning the validity of his own tradition. I think he shall help us a great deal. Already, he is reorganizing or reestablishing the old *tioshpaye*, a band or clan,[13] along the river here, and both he and Ben[14] are encouraging these people to take up again the old ways. The first thing they all say they shall do is to build the *Inipi* or Sweat Lodge, in the spring, and again use them with the correct rites. This band has already met several times for the old dances. During these dances almost everybody gives things away (this was once forbidden by law). Last week Theodore's grandmother gave me an old bow belonging to Fast Thunder, which he had used in hunting both buffalo and the whites. . . .

Tomorrow we shall finish the seventh and last rite, completing our history of the Sacred Pipe. I am extremely pleased the way this has turned out. . . . It is now time for me to leave, for I believe all has been done that can be at present, and I really think that many here have awakened to the glory of their heritage. All that prevents them from going ahead is their own inertia, which incidentally is very great among the majority of the people at this time. Our work on the book has done Ben much good, for bit by bit he has come to realize the truths that underlie his own rites; he is now even growing his hair long. I leave for Oraibi next week.

---

[13] Each Lakota is a member of a matrilineal clan, or *tioshpaye*. In pre-reservation days the Lakota camped with their clan, which was an extended family of close relatives who provided each member support in all practical matters.

[14] Benjamin Black Elk.

Last week, as I had long expected, we received a call from the local parish priest, who is also head of the mission school at Pine Ridge. He was quite irate about the pipe ceremonial, and said he did not mind if we merely wanted to put on a show, but if we were serious, it was a terrible thing, for he could not have his people going back to "savagery." At this Ben launched out with quite an oration, defending and pointing out the truths of his own tradition—during which time the priest became more and more tense and red in the face. When he finished, Old Black Elk started in, and went on for almost half an hour, after which the priest looked at his watch and sped off in his automobile in great haste. Black Elk's speech was later explained to me, and it was indeed a magnificent one. . . . The Catholic Church among the Indians in the early days gained many followers, by making catechists of the old men, tempting them with money, good clothes, and a house, and the opportunity to travel. These old men—Black Elk among them—made hundreds of converts, but now that they have gone, participation in the Church has fallen off, and a vacuum has been left. Let us hope it shall be filled by the renewal of their own Way. . . .

I have just come across an interesting point in connection with the tipi. All the poles except one are bound together. But this one free pole is used to set up the whole, and without it the tipi would fall apart. This unbound pole, which sustains the Universe, represents of course *Wakan-Tanka*, and it is on this that important offerings, sacred bundles, etc., are tied. The large tipis—for ceremonial purposes—have twenty-eight poles (mansions of the moon, and many other reasons, which will be explained in the book).

In Black Elk's home
January 27, 1948, Manderson, South Dakota
Yesterday Grandfather (Black Elk) and I went to visit Little Warrior again. Two means of action now seem to be well established:

1. In the spring, several holy men from each Sioux reservation shall meet to consider who is the most qualified to be the prospective keeper of the Pipe. Then they shall go to the Pipe, and it is quite possible that at this time it shall be unveiled, which as you know is possible in a crisis; and a crisis certainly does exist now.
2. It was agreed that the pipe of every old man be handed down to the most worthy of his descendants. This shall be good, for somehow these pipes have a way of getting into the museums, or into the hands of the profane whites.

Among the Hopi
February 4, 1948, Oraibi, Arizona
The most magnificent Introduction[15] arrived just a few days before I
left Manderson. Yes, it shall be a bitter pill for the ethnologists, but
that is just what is needed at this time. Parts of it were read to Black
Elk, and he was, of course, extremely pleased.

February 7 (continued in the same letter)
I was greeted here most warmly by Thomas Jenkins, his wife, and
two young children. He is one of those who was forced to go to the
government schools. It is difficult to fully realize the horror of these
places and the quality of the *shudras*[16] who teach there). His hair
was cut and he was given by them the name he now unfortunately
bears. He told me that he shall soon change it, for his real name is:
Banyacya, "Walking from the Waters," and he belongs to the Coyote
Clan, having received however only the first and lowest initiation, that
of the Kachina Society. He has an absolutely clear understanding of the
present crisis, and all that it signifies, although this is something he has
only recently understood, due in large part to the present war. He has
seen his own doctrine and Hopi prophecies being fulfilled.[17]

Hotevilla (Hota: "scrub cedar," Villa: "sloping rock") is a branch
of the old Oraibi which is the oldest continuously inhabited village of
the U.S.A., going back to 1000 or earlier, and is regarded, I understand,
as the capital or center of all the Pueblos of the Southwest. Those who
wished to retain their traditional life completely, were forced to leave
Oraibi by the "progressives," and founded with great difficulty Hotevilla in 1906. It is situated on the edge of a high and magnificent mesa;
below it is a spring from which all water is carried up, and along the
sides of the mesa they have then terraced gardens and fruit trees. The
entire setting is magnificent.

The two chiefs, Ponyawima, who is the head and belongs to the
Massawu Spirit Clan, and Katchgonva, who belongs to the Sun Clan,
have all along refused to cooperate or rather compromise with the

---

[15] The "Introduction" to the French edition of *The Sacred Pipe*.

[16] This is the Sanskrit word for the lowest caste of people.

[17] From 1949 until his death in 1999 Thomas Banyacya was the official spokesperson
for the spiritual elders of the Hopi tribe. Banyacya's first official address on behalf
of all Hopi elders is reprinted in *Indian Spirit*, edited by Michael Fitzgerald (World
Wisdom, 2003). Banyacya also became a well-known and respected spiritual leader
for his tribe.

government and with all that modern civilization represents. Under tremendous pressure and hardship they have been able to preserve almost miraculously, it seems, their whole traditional way of life, and possess, quite intact, their complete ritual cycle. But as is inevitable in these times, there is in Hotevilla a group of "progressives" who cause much trouble for the chiefs; but the latter have told me if necessary, they are quite prepared to move once again if they must.

After a visit to the Hopi, the Navajo, and the Pueblo
March 12, 1948, Aiken, South Carolina

At the beginning of the cycle, the Great Spirit gave to the Hopi two rock "maps," a sacred geography. One map defined the boundaries of the Hopi territory, of which the Grand Canyon is the center, or Place of Emergence. The other rock map has sacred writing on it, which, according to their beliefs, only the Great White Brother shall be able to read when He comes. The implications of possessing this sacred object at this particular time is of extreme importance.

The Navajo have many of the characteristics of the Plains Indians—qualities common to a more nomadic life—a spontaneous generosity, and spontaneous response to everything, a virility, freedom from the limiting conditions of space and time, lack of suspicion, etc.; qualities found not so much among the Pueblos, who tend to be close, more rigid, and private.

The governor of the Pueblo of Zuni in New Mexico is Leopoldo J. Eriacho—a very pleasant person, and more politically minded than anything else. He has fought well for his people and has done much to prevent the white encroachment and control. The religious leader of the Pueblo, with whom I stayed, is a charming old man: Chief Owaleon (Nash). He is also their war chief, which was hard to understand because of his very shy, gentle, reserved nature. He and his family received me well, insisted that I eat and sleep with them in their house, and were very eager to hear of my reason for being there. One thing became quite clear: they know the modern world's position in the present cycle of creation, and are determined to stick to their traditional way of life. Their ceremonial cycle is almost complete. When I left, they gave me a very beautiful silver and turquoise ring, and stressed the fact that they wished to hear from us often. (Incidentally, I might mention here that I have tried to keep in touch by letter with all the contacts we have made, for I realize how important this is. It has been a bit difficult while traveling, but I hope to catch up.) . . .

I have been hoping to do an article on the Ghost Dance—mostly to clarify, and to act as a corrective to Mooney (14th Annual Report, Bureau of Ethnology 1892-93, pt.2), who curiously enough saw the similarity with the dervish[18] dances, yet of course never understood the true nature of the ceremony, nor the end. Perhaps I shall not have time for it? The Pipe is the first in importance! . . .

Do not worry about any American Indian being "browbeaten" by the priests. Once their course of action is clear and set, nothing can turn them aside. He Holds the Lance left the Catholic school at the 8th grade because the priests denounced his own tradition, which he loved so well, and because the priests taught so many things which he knew to be untrue. Similarly, Chief Joseph of the Nez Perce, when asked by the Commissioner whether his tribe wanted schools, answered "No!" because "They will teach us to have churches, and churches will teach us to quarrel about God, as the Protestants and Catholics do on the Nez Perce reservation and at other places. . . . We may quarrel with men sometimes about things on this earth, but we never quarrel about God. We do not want to learn that" (*Building America*, Vol. VII, No. 4, 1940).

In Black Elk's home
Late summer 1948 (exact date unknown), Manderson, South Dakota
. . . About six months ago Little Warrior's grandson died of tuberculosis, after which they gave away all their possessions. Mrs. Little Warrior cut her hair short and made the *hanblecheyapi*[19] upon a mountain top. Little Warrior vowed at that time to make the retreat later in the summer, and did so when I was at his home last month. Incidentally his house shows an amazing detachment from the things of this world, for not only can you see the heavens above when inside, but you must walk upon the "floor" with great care lest you fall through one of the many holes. The family doesn't seem to notice these small details, and they are always happy singing, smoking, and praying, and never in any other home have I been cared for with greater attention and consideration.

Several days before the retreat, Little Warrior's friends and relatives began to arrive in their huge wagons and teams, and were followed by countless dogs—probably destined for some future feast. The women spent their time making hundreds of little tobacco bags to

[18] This is a reference to the dances of the "whirling dervishes" of Sufism.

[19] Vision quest.

be used as offerings, and others gathered the wild plums which were very plentiful along the rivers. They also crushed the dried cherries with rocks to make *wasna*, which the lamenter takes with him to the mountaintop.

I found it interesting to note the enthusiasm and respect all the people show, even the young, to the one making the retreat, for this in itself is proof that the tradition is far from dead.

Two nights before the retreat, Little Warrior held his *Yuwipi* rites, as mysterious and extraordinary as ever. Rattles and drums rushed about the room in the darkness, and gave out sparks as they hit the walls or floor. This was combined with powerful chanting—almost shrieking—of their *wakan* songs. It was at this time that I learnt that Little Warrior had vowed to make the retreat for several days and not with the rite which Black Elk had described to us.[20] Instead, he would be left within a rectangular sacred place with his fingers, hands, arms and feet tightly bound—a form which apparently is quite commonly used in these times. His relatives, however, urged him to consider his age and health (he nearly died last winter with a stroke), and not to make the retreat so difficult. After consulting with the "spirits" he agreed to make the fast for only a day and a night, and not to be tied up.

The next day he spent in preparation, fasting, and praying, and that afternoon we all entered the purification Sweat Lodge where we sang and steamed in very intense heat for almost half an hour. Afterwards, Little Warrior told me that he would like me to go with him and the women to the retreat site to see how the sacred place was made on the mountain top. This was done by first making a bed of sage stretching from West to East, and a rock placed at the West for a pillow. Blue, white, red, and yellow offering flags were placed at the four quarters around the bed, forming a rectangle, and bags of tobacco were tied as offerings to each pole. Three long strings were fastened to the poles from the South, West, North, and to East, thus leaving an opening on the side East to South. A hundred little bags of tobacco were tied to each of the three strings. An eagle feather was tied to a cherry stick representing the tree of life, which was stuck in the ground beside the

---

[20] This is a reference to the fact that the form of the Vision quest rite, *hanblecheyapi*, described by Black Elk and presented in *The Sacred Pipe* differs in various details from the form of the rite used by Little Warrior. The rite described by Black Elk is the basic rite performed by most Lakota. The rite described by Little Warrior is particular to those Lakota who possess *Yuwipi* medicine.

stone pillow. Beside it they placed a wooden bowl of *wasna* (Little Warrior had insisted that the bowl not be metal).

Little Warrior then approached the sacred place, wearing only a breach cloth and a blanket, and holding his huge pipe, addressed prayers to each of the directions. As he did so, the women and I moved so as to be always standing behind him. He then entered the sacred place, and the string of tobacco bags was tied behind him. He began to wail and cry pitifully, and we all left him and returned home with the sunset.

That night we all spent praying and singing. Often everybody would go outside in the dark and look towards the mountain where Little Warrior was, to see if there were any signs in that direction, and once, everybody became very excited when they saw a flash of lightning over the mountain, even though the night was clear and cold. They were also pleased the next morning when I spotted an eagle circling over the place. Then a few of us went up to bring him back, more dead than alive—or so it seemed—and I had to carry him to where the wagon was waiting. Upon our return we immediately entered the *Inipi* (sweat) lodge, and the heat seemed to revive him very quickly. When the rites of the *Inipi* were finished Little Warrior entered the house, and was greeted by everybody as if he had returned from the dead. His large pipe was smoked by all, and a feast followed.

I found it quite wonderful to observe the great care and love Little Warrior showed in doing perfectly the very smallest ritual acts—his eagle eyes were always watching everywhere, and if someone made a single move which was not ritually exact, he would be corrected immediately.

Later Little Warrior told me that he could not yet tell anybody what had happened to him during the retreat, but he did say that the four Powers had come to him during the retreat, and had given to him a new medicine—it was for curing tuberculosis. . . .

After a summer spent traveling to different American Indian reservations[21]
October 8, 1954, Albuquerque, New Mexico
In early July we arrived in Flagstaff, Arizona, where for three nights, by the lights of huge fires, some seventy nations celebrated their cere-

---

[21] This was an extended trip over the course of the entire summer that introduced Dr. Brown's new Swiss bride, Elenita, to the American West and to Brown's many American Indian friends.

monial dances. This was the best celebration that I have ever seen. The tourist atmosphere was almost completely annulled by the presence of some 10,000 Navajo camped around the dancing area. After having been in the East for almost a year, I really felt at home once again. It is clear to me now, that as long as we live in the States we must be somewhere in this Western country near the Indians. After the dances one night we had a good visit in the tent of the Oglala Sioux from Pine Ridge, and it was from them that I learned of the Sioux Sun Dance on July 28th at Pine-Ridge. . . .

As we traveled north, we were fortunate to arrive among the Shoshone during their Sun Dance.[22] We had several conversations with John Trehero, the Sun Dance chief of the Shoshone. He is an unusual man in appearance and behavior, yet if you observe him closely you can feel something of his power behind his disarming appearance.

After the dance I heard of an amazing cure, which he had worked there. A man had been X-rayed at the hospital and had been found to have a very severe case of gallstones—so severe that they wished to operate immediately. But the man wished to attend the Sun Dance, and so they let him go after the man promised to return immediately afterwards. At the dance, however, Trehero "worked" on him with his feathers and prayer, and when the man got up he found a pile of stones under him where he had been lying, and he felt completely well. He returned to the hospital where they were prepared to operate on him, and not believing him when he said he was quite well, they again X-rayed, and indeed found that the gallstones had disappeared. Later among the Crow, I heard of many more such miraculous cures which John had worked.

After the Sun Dance I visited Trehero in his tipi. We talked of many things concerning the Sun Dance and how he brought it to the Crow.[23] He asked me if I had noticed that the dance stopped at noon when the sun is straight up. He then explained that this is the sacred time, for the sun will stay straight up when "the end of the world comes" and this time was not far off.

---

[22] The Shoshone Sun Dance in question took place in Fort Washakie, Wyoming.

[23] There are two books that make many references to Trehero and to the history of Trehero bringing the form of the Shoshone Sun Dance to the Crow tribe: *The Shoshoni-Crow Sun Dance*, edited by Fred Voget (University of Oklahoma Press, 1984) and *Yellowtail: Crow Medicine Man and Sun Dance Chief*, recorded and edited by Michael Fitzgerald (University of Oklahoma Press, 1991).

Trehero looks as much Mexican as Shoshone. He wears a big black hat and black shirt with a huge white scarf. If one watches his eyes one has the impression of much cleverness combined with power. He is not old—possibly 55-60.[24] He loves to joke and tell funny stories. While watching him at a camp circle later, at Sheridan and again at the Crow Agency, I noticed he would make the rounds, visiting and laughing with everybody, and he never passes a child without saying something to him. Once, at Sheridan, he came up to me and said that he had been thinking of our talk together and it made him very happy. . . .

Later in Black Hills we met Ben Black Elk and his family again, and for three days we had a very happy time together. Often there would be up to twenty visitors at one time in their little house. They would come from other reservations and would sing and drum late into the night. Ben seemed stronger to me than before, and I think sincerely glad to see us; they certainly accepted us into the family as one of them. . . .

It was good to be back at Pine Ridge and to see all the people gathered together for the Sun Dance—some 400 tents. But it was sad to see the way in which the Sun Dance was done, and also to note that none of the young Sioux did the dance—only the young Cheyenne led by two old Sioux priests—good men—but not of the quality of a Little Warrior. These Cheyenne were veterans and had vowed during the Korean War to do the Sun Dance many times should they return safely. They had already danced twice that summer, and would do it more among other nations. They seemed very pleased after the dance when I gave them a copy of *The Sacred Pipe*. The ritual aspect of the Sun Dance was rather laxly done, as it was held in conjunction with two days of "social dancing," which consisted largely of the "Omaha" war dance in which almost everybody participated.[25] The Sun Dance starts at sunrise each day, but ends in the afternoon. After a short break the social dancing starts in the same location and lasts into the night. Both the Sun Dance and the social dances were very powerful

---

[24] In 1954 Trehero was 70 years old.

[25] A detailed account of the history of the Lakota Sun Dance during the twentieth century is contained in *Fools Crow*, recorded by Thomas Mails (insert most recent edition). Fools Crow was Black Elk's nephew and one of the most important Lakota Sun Dance chiefs of the twentieth century. In 1952 the government gave Fools Crow permission to lead an authentic Sun Dance in conjunction with the annual summer Pine Ridge Fair and Pow-wow. The Sun Dance had to be stopped each afternoon to allow the pow-wow dancing. It was only during the 1960s that the public Sun Dance at Pine Ridge was held separately from the pow-wows.

and even now I can still hear those drums (they had five different teams of drummers), and those incredibly strong and beautiful songs and chants. I have a special affinity for the Sioux tribe. . . .

Our first meeting with Thomas and Susie Yellowtail[26] and the Crow friends was at Sheridan. We were certainly very warmly received and arranged to meet them later on the reservation. When we arrived on the Crow reservation we found that the family had unexpectedly gone north, 300 miles to the Assiniboine reservation for a big dance, so we too went north and camped with them for five days. Here I met a fine old Assiniboine priest—Standing One—one of the last of these old men, I was told. I was very pleased when he agreed to bless a large pipe which I had purchased among the Sioux. In his presence I felt that I was with Black Elk once again. At this time the old man was transferring his power to a Cree, Hollers, who had come down from Saskatchewan.

There were many Cree at this dance, and they had brought with them an account which was being told all over the camp and which pleased the old men a great deal. Sometime in this summer an old Cree woman from northern Saskatchewan died. On the fourth day they prepared her for burial, and all the relatives cut their hair and mourned for her as was the custom. On the fourth day, however, the woman came to life and spoke to the people around her. She told them that she had returned in order to bring them an important message. First, when a person died, we should not mourn, for the place to which she had been is far more beautiful than it is here on earth. Secondly, she explained that she had been sent back to tell the Indian people that, although they should respect the religion of the whites, they should follow in their own religion to the end. For the white people have caused so much mischief in the world that they are soon to have a great punishment, and Indians who follow the ways of the whites will receive this punishment too. Further, she said, those who hear this message are obliged to pass it on to another. After saying this to her people, the old lady died. This account, it seems, is now being told and retold all over the northern reservations, and it cannot but bring much good. Later, on the Crow reservation, I noticed old men retelling this account in sign language.

---

[26] Thomas Yellowtail's life and role in perpetuating the Crow Sun Dance is contained in *Yellowtail: Crow Medicine Man and Sun Dance Chief*, recorded and edited by Michael Fitzgerald (University of Oklahoma Press, 1991). Susie Yellowtail was the first Native American nurse, a tireless advocate of the traditional values of the Crow, and is enshrined in the Montana Hall of Fame in the State Capital Building in Helena.

After this dance we returned to Wyola, Tom and Susie Yellowtail's home on the Crow reservation, where we spent two weeks visiting with them. Their farm is very beautiful at the foot of the Big Horn Mountains and by the Little Big Horn river in which we swam almost twice a day. One night we participated in their monthly Sun Dance prayer ceremony, which they gave especially for their son Bruce, who had just returned from Korea. Throughout the war he had carried with him protective feathers given to him by John Trehero and he was now returning these feathers to the family sacred bundle. Once Tom and I had the *Inipi* bath by the river—the longest I have ever had—almost two hours. It was good to do this with him and it was here that he was really seen at his best. . . .

Our travels of this summer have been of tremendous value to us. For almost two months we heard the powerful rhythms of the big drums almost continually, as we went from one dance to another—and even now I can still hear them, for it seems that they have become a part—or more than a part—of me. I know that somehow my lot is tied up with that of the Indians. In what way this is to be worked out is still to be seen, but I know that I must have confidence that the step that I am now taking will lead towards some solution of the question.

BIOGRAPHY OF JOSEPH E. BROWN

Dr. Brown was a renowned scholar, author, and teacher of Native American Traditions and World Religions. Joseph believed that all great world religions are paths that lead ultimately to the same summit, and dedicated his life to bring Native American Religions into the canon of World Religions. Through his teaching, writing, and friendships he served as a vital bridge, promoting understanding between Native American and White cultures.

Joseph was born in Ridgefield Connecticut, September 9, 1920. He spent his youth in Aiken, South Carolina and Southwest Harbor, Maine, where he enjoyed sailing, hunting, and horsemanship. It was in Maine that he was first exposed to Native American cultures and as a young boy made friendships with the *Wabanaki*, who taught him how to fish and hunt. These friendships were the beginning of his lifelong interest in American Indian spirituality.

As a young boy he attended boarding school in Aiken, South Carolina, and Asheville, North Carolina. A rebellious student, he kept his hunting gun hidden under his mattress and his bird dog at a nearby farm. He would spend his weekends hunting and roaming the countryside with his dog. During his early teens, his father developed tuberculosis and was sent to a sanatorium in New Mexico. Joseph would spend his summer vacations there, riding and exploring. This was his first exposure to the American West, where he would later return to spend the majority of his life. His father died of tuberculosis when Joseph was 17.

Joseph's undergraduate college education began at Bowdoin College (B.A. in Literature) and then continued at Haverford College (B.A. in Philosophy and Art History). He then postponed his graduate study and took his first teaching post at Aiken Preparatory School in South Carolina teaching English.

During World War II, Joseph chose to become a Conscientious Objector. In the early part of the war he washed bottles in a drab malaria research lab/morgue in New York City. Seeking to feed his spirit during this dark time he studied the sacred forms of different religions. To learn more fully about Christianity he took Gregorian chant lessons; and to learn more fully about Islam he befriended Yemeni sailors at the Brooklyn docks. They would dance *Hadrats* (sacred Islamic chants and dances) in the holds of the ships. Later during the war Joseph was shipped out to Nevada and California in a sealed railroad car, where he was relieved to perform civilian duty packing mules, clearing trails, and surveying the depth of the snow pack for the Forest Service.

After the war, in the late 1940s, Joseph outfitted an old truck into living quarters and traveled west to seek out the Lakota Sioux holy man, Black Elk. He had read about this holy man in Neihardt's *Black Elk Speaks* and was determined to meet him. He found Black Elk and his family in the fall of 1947, living in tents, picking potatoes in Nebraska. Black Elk, nearly blind, was expecting him, and invited Joseph to return with him to their home in Manderson, South Dakota. He lived with Black Elk and his family on the Pine Ridge Reservation for several years, during which time Black Elk adopted him as a son. He was given the Sioux name *Channumpa Yuha Mani* or "He Who Walks with the Sacred Pipe." During that time he recorded Black Elk's account of the seven rites of the Oglala Sioux, later published as the well-known book *The Sacred Pipe* (University of Oklahoma Press), an enduring and seminal record of Plains Indian religious expression, still in print today and translated into eight languages.

In addition to *The Spiritual Legacy of the American Indian* (originally published by Crossroad Publishing), and *The Sacred Pipe*, Joseph has also authored *Animals of the Soul: Sacred Animals of the Oglala Sioux* (Element Books), and *Teaching Spirits: Understanding Native American Religious Traditions* (Oxford University Press). A *Festschrift* honoring Joseph's life and work is currently being prepared for publication.[1]

In 1952, Joseph married Swiss dancer and artist Elenita Roulet in Switzerland. Joseph returned to the United States with his new bride where they lived on the Maine coast while Joseph prepared *The Sacred Pipe* for publication and Elenita studied pottery. The couple then moved to Albuquerque, New Mexico, where Joseph pursued a Master's degree in Anthropology at the University of New Mexico, and his wife studied art and Flamenco dance. Disillusioned by the dry and scientific anthropological approach to Native American cultures during that time, Joseph eventually left graduate school. The couple then taught at Verde Valley School, a groundbreaking alternative private high school in Sedona, Arizona, where children Alexander and Marina were born. During a sabbatical, Joseph lived in Safi, Morocco, where he taught English and studied Arabic, and where daughter Malika was born. After Morocco the couple returned to Verde Valley School where their fourth child, Veronica, was born.

---

[1] A complete bibliography is presented in the section entitled the Published Works of Joseph E. Brown.

Joseph completed his M.A. in Anthropology at Stanford University in 1966. Joseph and Elenita taught at Prescott College in Arizona prior to moving to Sweden in 1969, where he received a Doctorate in Anthropology and History of Religions from the University of Stockholm under the tutelage of renowned scholar Åke Hultkrantz. His close relationship with Hultkrantz was to last for the remainder of his life.

In 1970, Dr. Brown created the first Native American Religious Studies program in the United States at Indiana University, Bloomington, where he remodeled a farm in the wooded countryside in order to have his beloved horses close at hand. A natural horseman, Joseph had a lifelong love and knowledge of horses. In the fall of 1972, he joined the Religious Studies faculty at the University of Montana, Missoula, where he taught until his retirement in 1989. On his ranch outside of Missoula at the foot of the Bitterroot Mountains he raised and trained Arabian horses. Joseph's love and respect for the American buffalo (bison) resulted in the establishment of a small breeding herd of bison at the ranch. His daughter, Malika B. Coston, continues his horsemanship legacy today at the family ranch.

Dr. Brown was well loved and respected by his students. In his quiet, eclectic, and dignified manner he combined humor, storytelling, and the arts into his teaching. The reciprocity and relatedness of all life was a major theme in his classrooms and he emulated what he taught.

During his professional teaching career, Joseph was also contributing editor for many years to numerous publications including *Parabola*, *The Handbook of Living Religions*, and *The Encyclopedia of Religion*. He lectured extensively throughout the world during his career, established and chaired the first "Indigenous Religious Traditions Group" of the American Academy of Religion and was often invited to testify for Native American Tribes in court cases in defense of the Freedom of Religion Act. Joseph was a sought-after book reviewer and consultant, advisor and consultant for film, and advisor to American Indian prisoners.

In 1984 Joseph was a founding director of the Foundation for Traditional Studies, a non-profit foundation dedicated to "preserving and strengthening the religious traditions which have been transmitted through the ages and which have so much to teach contemporary society." The mission statement for the foundation's journal, *Sophia*, states that it is "the foremost journal in the field of traditional studies in the English language." Joseph was a director of the foundation and an editorial board member of the journal for the remainder of his life.

Joseph passed away in 2000, at the age of 80, at his home in Stevensville after a long illness. He was surrounded and loved by his wife, four children, four grandchildren, many four-leggeds and the Bitterroot Mountains.

His close friend, the eminent scholar Seyyed Hossein Nasr, wrote a tribute to Joseph in *Sophia* shortly after Brown's death that concluded with this opinion: "America has not produced another scholar of the Native American traditions who combined in himself, as did Joseph Brown, profound spiritual and intellectual insight and traditional understanding, the deepest empathy for those traditions, nobility of character and generosity towards his students and everyone else who wanted to benefit from his unrivalled knowledge of the spiritual legacy of the first inhabitants of this continent."

With the sensitivity of a poet, the rationality of a scholar, and the light and love of a spiritual seeker, Dr. Brown's work lives on and continues to uncover for us the abundant resources for modern human survival found in the American Indian heritage.

PUBLISHED WORKS OF JOSEPH E. BROWN

BOOKS

——*The Sacred Pipe: Black Elk's Account of the Seven Rites of the Oglala Sioux.* Norman: University of Oklahoma Press, 1953, 1989; New York: Penguin Books, 1971.
TRANSLATIONS:
—*Les Rites Secrets des Indians Sioux.* Paris: Payot, 1953.
—*Die Heilige Pfeife.* Olten: Walter-Verlag, 1956.
—*La Sacra Pipa.* Torino: Borla Editore, 1970; *La Pipa Sagrata.* Torino: Casa Editrice G. Einaudi, 1977, 2005.
—*The Sacred Pipe.* Stockholm: Swedish Writers Press, 1978.
—*De heilige pijp.* Utrecht: Bijleveld B.V., 1998.
—*La Pipa Sagrada.* Madrid: Miraguano Ediciones, 1993, 1996, 2002.
—Hungarian edition of *The Sacred Pipe*, 2004.
—Japanese edition of *The Sacred Pipe*, forthcoming.
——*The Spiritual Legacy of the American Indian* (pamphlet). New York: Pendle Hill, 1964-1976.
——*The North American Indians: The Photographs of Edward S. Curtis.* New York: Aperture, 1972.
——*The Spiritual Legacy of the American Indian.* New York: Crossroad Publishing Co., 1982; *Commemorative Edition with Letters While Living with Black Elk,* Bloomington, IN: World Wisdom, 2007.
TRANSLATIONS:
—*L'Héritage Spirituel des Indiens d'Amérique.* Editions Le Mail, 1990.
——*The Gift of the Sacred Pipe: Based on Black Elk's Account of the Seven Rites of the Oglala Sioux.* With Vera Loise Drysdale. Norman: University of Oklahoma Press, 1982.
——*Animals of the Soul: Sacred Animals of the Oglala Sioux.* Rockport, MA: Element, 1992, 1997; London: Chrysalis Books, 2005.
TRANSLATIONS:
—*Animales del Alma. Animales sagrados de los Oglala Siux.* Palma de Mallorca: Ed. Olañeta, 1994.
—*Animali dell'anima, Animali sacred del Oglala Sioux.*
—*Dieren van de Ziel: Heilige Dieren van Oglala Sioux.*

131

——*Teaching Spirits: Understanding Native American Traditions* (with Emily Cousins). New York: Oxford University Press, 2001.

ARTICLES

"The Husbandman." In *Homage to Ananda Coomaraswamy: A Memorial Volume*, edited by S. Durai Raja Singam, Probsthain: Singapore, 1951.

"Les Miroirs Chinois." *Études Traditionnelles*. Paris, 1954.

"The Symbolical Forms in Chinese Mirrors." *Asia*, December 1954. (Reprinted for course text by the University of Michigan.)

L'Art du Tir a l'Arc." *Études Traditionnelles*. Paris, 1956.

"The Spiritual Legacy of the American Indian." *Tomorrow*, Autumn, vol. 12, no. 4, 1964.

"The Persistence of Essential Values Among North American Plains Indians." *Studies in Comparative Religion*, Autumn 1969. Reprinted in Sam Gill, *Native American Traditions*. Belmont, California: Wadsworth Publishers, 1983.

"The Unlikely Associates." *Studies in Comparative Religion*, Summer 1970; *Ethnos*. Stockholm, 1970.

"The Spiritual Legacy of the American Indian." In *Sources*, edited by Theodore Roszack. New York: Harper and Row, 1972.

"Modes of Contemplation Through Actions: North American Indians." In *Main Currents in Modern Thought*, Nov.-Dec. 1973.

"The Question of 'Mysticism' with Native American Traditions." In *Mystics and Scholars*, edited by Harold Coward and Ternece Penelhum. Waterloo: Wilfrid Laurier University Press, 1976.

"The Roots of Renewal." In *Seeing with a Native Eye*, edited by Walter Capps. New York: Harper and Row, 1976.

"On Being Human." In *The Religious Character of Native American Humanities*, edited by Sam Gill. Tempe: Arizona State University, 1977.

"Contemplation Through Actions: North American Indians." In *Contemplation and Action in World Religions*, edited by Yusuf Ibish and Lleana Marculescu. Huston: Rothko Chapel Books; distributed by University of Washington Press, 1978.

"Sun Dance: Sacrifice, Renewal, Identity." *Parabola*, May 1978. Reprinted in *Religion North American Style*, edited by Patrick H. McNamara. Belmont, California: Wadsworth Publishers, 1984.

"A Tribute to Paul Goble." *The Caldecott Medal Awards.* New York: Bradbury Press, Inc., 1979.

"Clown and *Hehoka* in Plains Indian Traditions." *Parabola*, February 1979.

"Introduction." In Bruce Walter Barton, *The Tree at the Center of the World: A Story of the California Missions.* Santa Barbara, Ross-Erickson Publishers, 1979.

"The Immediacy of Mythological Message." In *Native Religious Traditions*, edited by Earle H. Waugh and K Dad Prithipaul: Waterloo, Ont.: Wilfrid Laurier University Press for the Canadian Corp. for Studies in Religion, 1979.

"The Trickster in American Indian Traditions." Interview with Dorothy Dooling, *Parabola*, vol. IV, no. 1, 1979.

"Time and Process." In *The Responsibility of the Academic Community in the Search for Absolute Values*, proceedings of the Eighth International Conference on the Unity of the Sciences. New York: The International Cultural Foundations Press, 1980.

"The Bison and the Moth: Lakota Correspondences." *Parabola*, Spring 1983.

"North American Indian Religions." In *A Handbook of Living Religions*, edited by John R. Hinnels. London: Penguin Books, 1984.

"L'héritage spirituel des Indiens d'Amérique du Nord." *Connaissance des Religions*, September 1985.

"Persistance des Valeurs Essentielles chez les Indiens des Plaines d'Amérique du Nord." *Inter culture.* Montreal, Canada, Jan.-Mars 1985.

"Sun Dance," "Black Elk," "The Great Spirit," and "Lakota Religious Terms." In *The Encyclopedia of Religion*, edited by Mircea Eliade. New York: Macmillan Publishing Company, 1986.

"American Indian Experience." In *The Unanimous Tradition,* edited by Ranjit Fernando. Colombo: Sri Lanka Institute of Traditional Studies, 1992.

"The Sacred Language of Plains Indian Art Forms." In *In Quest of the Sacred: The Modern World in the Light of Tradition.* Edited by Katherine O'Brien and Seyyed Hossein Nasr. Foundation for Traditional Studies, VA, 1994

ACKNOWLEDGMENTS

Chapter 2: "The Spiritual Legacy" is reprinted by permission of Pendle Hill Publications from *The Spiritual Legacy of the American Indian* by Joseph Epes Brown, copyright © 1964 by Pendle Hill.

Chapter 3: "The Roots of Renewal" appeared in *Seeing With a Native Eye*, edited by Walter Holden Capps. Copyright © 1976 by Walter Holden Capps. Reprinted by permission of Harper & Row, Publishers, Inc.

Chapter 4: "The Persistence of Essential Values" was presented at the International Congress of the Instituto Accademico di Roma in 1968 and reprinted in *Conoscenga religiosa*, edited by Elémire Zolla.

Chapter 5: "Contemplation Through Action" appeared in *Contemplation and Action in World Religions*, edited by Yusuf Ibish and Lleana Marculescu, copyright © 1977, 1978 by the Rothko Chapel and the De Menil Foundation.

Chapter 6: "The Immediacy of Mythological Message" is reprinted with permission from Earle H. Waugh and K. Dad Prithipaul, editors, *Native Religious Traditions* (Waterloo, Ontario: Wilfrid University Press for the Canadian Corporation for Studies in Religion/Corporation Canadienne des Sciences Religieuses, 1979).

Chapter 7: "Sun Dance: Sacrifice, Renewal, Identity" originally appeared in *Parabola*, vol. 3, no. 2 (Sacrifice and Transformation). Used with permission.

Chapter 8: "The Question of 'Mysticism'" appeared in *Mystics and Scholars: The Calgary Conference on Mysticism, 1976*, edited by Harold Coward and Terence Penelhum, copyright © 1977 by the Canadian Corporation for Studies in Religion.

Chapter 9: "Time and Process" is reprinted from *The Responsibility of the Academic Community in the Search for Absolute Values*, Proceedings of the Eighth International Conference on the Unity of the Sciences (Los Angeles, 1979). By permission of the International Cultural

Chapter 10: "On Being Human" appeared in the booklet *The Religious Character of Native American Humanities: An Interdisciplinary Conference held April 14-16, 1977*, Department of Humanities and Religious Studies, Arizona State University, Tempe, Arizona.

Grateful acknowledgment is made to the following for permission to reprint previously published material:

The University of Oklahoma Press for excerpts from *The Sacred Pipe* by Joseph Epes Brown, copyright © 1953 by the University of Oklahoma Press.

The John G. Neihardt Trust for excerpts from *Black Elk Speaks* by John G. Neihardt, copyright © by John G. Neihardt, published by Simon & Schuster and the University of Nebraska Press.

PHOTOGRAPHIC CREDITS

Cover: "Black Elk, 1948," by Joseph Epes Brown.
Page ii: "Joseph Epes Brown and Black Elk, Pine Ridge, 1947," from the Joseph Brown family.

Photo Signature:

Page 1:   "Joseph Epes Brown in Pine Ridge, South Dakota, 1948," from the Joseph Brown family.
Page 2:   "Black Elk and wife, c. 1883," from World Wisdom's collection.
Page 3:   "Black Elk, 1948," by Joseph Epes Brown.
Page 4:   "Mrs. Little Warrior, Little Warrior, and Black Elk, 1948," by Joseph Epes Brown.
Page 5:   "Little Warrior, 1948," by Joseph Epes Brown.
Page 6:   "John Trehero outside a Shoshone Sun Dance, 1940s," by Åke Hultkrantz.
Page 7:   "Thomas Yellowtail outside a Crow Sun Dance, 1979," by Michael Oren Fitzgerald.
Page 8a: "Father Gall," from the Estate of Frithjof Schuon.
Page 8b: "Chief Dan Katchgonva, Hopi, Sun Clan, 1948," by Joseph Epes Brown.

BIOGRAPHICAL NOTES

MARINA BROWN WEATHERLY is a professional artist and educator. The oldest daughter of Joseph Epes Brown, Brown Weatherly has taught art at universities, public and private schools, and has conducted workshops for teachers. She is the co-director of Kootenai Creek Ranch, a summer day camp in Montana. She has also published several articles and is editing a forthcoming biography of the late Susie Walking Bear Yellowtail, the first American Indian nurse and wife of Crow Sun Dance chief Thomas Yellowtail.

ELENITA BROWN is a renowned dancer, teacher, and artist. Elenita was married to Joseph Epes Brown for nearly 50 years. Elenita has exhibited her artwork nationwide and has taught, choreographed, and performed various dance styles throughout her life. Joseph and Elenita have four grown children, Alexander, Marina, Malika, and Veronica. In addition to teaching and performing dance, Elenita continues to run Kootenai Creek Ranch with her family in Stevensville, Montana.

MICHAEL OREN FITZGERALD has edited or co-edited eleven books on world religions, which have received four prestigious awards, including "Best Book in Religion and Philosophy" for both 2004 and 2005 by the Midwest Independent Publisher's Association. Four of his books on American Indian spirituality are used in university classes. Fitzgerald has taught Religious Traditions of the North American Indians in the Indiana University Continuing Studies Department. Michael is also the adopted son of the late Thomas Yellowtail, one of the most honored American Indian spiritual leaders of the last century. He holds a Doctor of Jurisprudence from Indiana University. Fitzgerald was Joseph Brown's graduate teaching assistant at Indiana University for three semesters.

ÅKE HULTKRANTZ is recognized as a world authority on Native American religions and shamanism and was professor of religion at the University of Stockholm. During the years 1948 and 1958, Professor Hultkrantz conducted fieldwork in the American West that resulted in his groundbreaking book, *Native American Religions of North America: The Power of Visions and Fertility*, first published in 1987. His books include *The Religions of the American Indians, Shamanic Healing and Ritual Drama: Health and Medicine in the Native North American Religious Traditions*, and *Belief and Worship in Native America*. Professor Hultkrantz died in October 2006.

INDEX

For a glossary of all key foreign words used in books published by World Wisdom, including metaphysical terms in English, consult: www.DictionaryofSpiritualTerms.org.
This on-line Dictionary of Spiritual Terms provides extensive definitions, examples and related terms in other languages.

World Wisdom's Other American Jndian Titles

*All Our Relatives: Traditional Native American
Thoughts about Nature*
compiled and illustrated by Paul Goble, 2005

*The Essential Charles Eastman (Ohiyesa):
Light on the Indian World*
edited by Michael Oren Fitzgerald, 2007

The Feathered Sun: Plains Indians in Art and Philosophy
by Frithjof Schuon, 1990

The Gospel of the Redman: Commemorative Edition
compiled by Ernest Thompson Seton and Julia M. Seton, 2005

Indian Spirit: Revised and Enlarged
edited by Judith Fitzgerald and Michael Oren Fitzgerald, 2006

Native Spirit: The Sun Dance Way by Thomas Yellowtail
edited by Michael Oren Fitzgerald, 2007

The Spirit of Indian Women
edited by Judith Fitzgerald and Michael Oren Fitzgerald, 2005

Tipi: Home of the Nomadic Buffalo Hunters
compiled and illustrated by Paul Goble, 2007

Films about American Jndian Spirituality by World Wisdom

Native Spirit & The Sun Dance Way
produced by Michael Oren Fitzgerald,
directed by Jennifer Casey, 2007